WORKBOOK

BIG
ENGLISH 3

Mario Herrera • **Christopher Sol Cruz**

Big English
Workbook 3

Pearson Education, 10 Bank Street, White Plains, NY 10606 USA

Staff credits: The people who made up the **Big English** team, representing editorial, production, design, manufacturing, and marketing are Rhea Banker, Danielle Belfiore, Carol Brown, Tracey Munz Cataldo, Daniel Comstock, Mindy DePalma, Dave Dickey, Gina DiLillo, Christine Edmonds, Nancy Flaggman, Yoko Mia Hirano, Caroline Kasterine, Amy Kefauver, Lucille Kennedy, Penny Laporte, Christopher Leonowicz, Emily Lippincott, Maria Pia Marrella, Jennifer McAliney, Kate McLoughlin, Julie Molnar, Linda Moser, Kyoko Oinuma, Leslie Patterson, Sherri Pemberton, Pamela Pia, Stella Reilly, Mary Rich, Nicole Santos, Susan Saslow, Donna Schaffer, Chris Siley, Kim Snyder, Heather St. Clair, Mairead Stack, Katherine Sullivan, Jane Townsend, Kenneth Volcjak, and Lauren Weidenman.

Contributing writer: Teresa Lintner

Text composition: Bill Smith Group/Q2A Media

Illustration credits: Q2A Media Services, Remy Simard, Tiago Americo

Photo credits: Cover/Title Page (bc) Kidstock/Getty Images; 3 (tr) Mau Horng/Shutterstock, (tcr) 4Max/Shutterstock, (cr) DenisNata/Fotolia, (bcr) sveta/Fotolia, (br) Fabian Petzold/Fotolia; 5 (tr) MaszaS/Shutterstock; 6 (cr) Monkey Business Images/Dreamstime; 7 (tl) Ene/Dreamstime, (tr) Gyorgy/Dreamstime, (cl) Cheryl Casey/Getty Images, (cr) Dave Nagel/Getty Images, (bl) Rmarmion/Dreamstime, (br) Stuart Miles/Shutterstock; 8 (tr) Smileus/Shutterstock, (tcr) hartphotography/Shutterstock, (cr) Subbotina Anna/Fotolia, (c) Corbis Flirt/Alamy, (bcr) Pete Pahham/Shutterstock, (bc) Cultura Creative/Alamy, (br) JPagetRMphotos/Alamy; 9 (tr) Monkey Business Images/Dreamstime, (cr) Odua/Dreamstime; 11 (tl) Corbis RF/Alamy, (tcl) PhotoAlto sas/Alamy, (bcl) Vasaleks/Shutterstock, (bl) moodboard Premium/Fotolia; 12 (tr) erwinova/Shutterstock, (c) Erasmus Wolff/Shutterstock, (bl) Rob Marmion/Shutterstock, (br) Yobro10/Dreamstime, (b) Yuri Arcurs/Fotolia; 16 (tr) Blend Images/Superstock, (br) Matthew Jacques/Shutterstock; 18 (tc) Pressureua/Dreamstime, (tcr) Ryan McGinnis/AgeFotostock, (tr) illustrart/Shutterstock; 19 (tl) NaughtyNut/Shutterstock, (tl inset) Odua/Dreamstime, (tcr) PHOTOCREO Michal Bednarek/Shutterstock, (tcr inset) Erika Cross/Shutterstock, (cl) OJO Images Ltd/Alamy; 21 (tl) erwinova/Shutterstock, (tcl) Lisa F. Young/Shutterstock, (tcr) Erasmus Wolff/Shutterstock, (tr) Directphoto/Alamy, (bl) Jeanne McRight/Fotolia, (bcl) Yobro10/Dreamstime, (bc) RobMattingley/iStock, (cr) fStop/Alamy, (br) Tyler Olson/Shutterstock; 22 (tc) auremar/Shutterstock, (tr) Juanmonino/iStockphoto, (bc) auremar/Shutterstock, (bc) Sebastian Czapnik/Dreamstime; 23 (br) Image_Source/iStockphoto; 25 (ball) DenisNata/Fotolia, (books) Odua/Dreamstime, (wheelchair) andres balcazar/iStockphoto, (piano) Akeeris/Dreamstime, (bed making) Tetra Images/Alamy; 28 (piggy bank) Robyn Mackenzie/Shutterstock; 29 (tl) Ints/Fotolia, (cl) LindaYolanda/iStockphoto, (bl) Deco/Alamy; 31 (tl) MIXA/Alamy, (tr) Akeeris/Dreamstime, (br) MBI/Alamy; 34 (tl) panbazil/Shutterstock, (tr) Stephen Frink Collection/Alamy, (cr) Wild Geese/Fotolia, (bl) Dmytro Pylypenko/Shutterstock, (br) Sean Cameron/Alamy; 37 (tc) Rich Carey/Shutterstock, (tr) Poco_bw/Dreamstime, (tcr) Bigmax/Dreamstime, (cr) STEVE LINDRIDGE/Alamy, (bcr) Sobek85/Dreamstime, (br) Tischenko Irina/Shutterstock; 39 (tr) Itinerantlens/Dreamstime; 40 (tl) Wtshi/Dreamstime, (tc) Ukrphoto/Dreamstime, (tr) Marjanvisserphotography/Dreamstime; 41 (tl) Jacek Chabraszewski/Fotolia, (tr) Tischenko Irina/Shutterstock, (tcl) OJO Images Ltd/Alamy, (tcr) Devonyu/Dreamstime, (bcl) Erika Cross/Shutterstock, (bcr left) Eric Isselée/Shutterstock, (bcr right) Susan Schmitz/Shutterstock, (bl) Odua/Dreamstime, (br) Photowitch/Dreamstime; 42 (tr) Myrleen Pearson/Alamy; 43 (bkgnd) Volina/Shutterstock, (tl) airn/Shutterstock, (tr) Volodymyr Krasyuk/Shutterstock, (tcl) Ultrashock/Shutterstock, (tcr) cellistka/Shutterstock, (bl) Valentyna Chukhlyebova/Shutterstock, (bc) Istomina Olena/Shutterstock, (br) Rich Carey/Shutterstock; 44 (tl) Jaypmorgan/Dreamstime, (tr) Monkey Business Images/Dreamstime, (bl) Peter Phipp/Travelshots.com/Alamy, (br) Robert Hoetink/Shutterstock; 47 (tr) iofoto/Fotolia; 50 (tl) yashar61/iStockphoto, (tr) Sergey Toronto/Shutterstock, (bl) Photoshot Holdings Ltd/Alamy, (br) Ingrid Petitjean/Shutterstock; 51 (tc) Zero Creatives Cultura/Newscom, (bl) Ulrich Doering/Alamy, (br) Chunghwa/Dreamstime; 52 (tl) artcasta/Shutterstock, (tr) Pierre-Yves Babelon/Shutterstock; 53 (bl) Peter Phipp/Travelshots/Alamy, (br) Kotenko Oleksandr/Shutterstock; 54 (tr) Mat Hayward/Shutterstock, (tr inset) sniegirova mariia/Shutterstock; 58 (tl) Xalanx/Dreamstime, (tr) Armadillo Stock/Shutterstock, (bcl) GekaSkr/Shutterstock, (br) Jag_cz/Shutterstock, (bl) Ljupco Smokovski/Shutterstock; 60 (tl) kwokfai/Shutterstock, (tc) Eric Isselée/Shutterstock, (tr) Cathy Keifer/Shutterstock; 61 (tl) Ljupco Smokovski/Shutterstock, (tr) Diego Cervo/Shutterstock, (bl) Dan Bannister/AgeFotostock, (br) Michael Snell/Robert Harding/Newscom; 62 (br) Bigmax/Dreamstime; 63 (tl) Blend Images/SuperStock, (tcl) ispstock/Fotolia, (c) yashar61/iStockphoto, (bcl) HomeArt/Shutterstock, (bl) Glow Images Inc/Getty Images; 65 (tc) Sobek85/Dreamstime, (tr) Poco_bw/Dreamstime, (c) Rich Carey/Shutterstock; 66 (tr) Blend Images/SuperStock, (br) Blend Images/SuperStock; 69 (ham) Sundebo/Shutterstock, (mushroom) Andrjuss/Shutterstock, (pickles) Scruggelgreen/Dreamstime, (sausage) cosma/Shutterstock, (pepper) James Harrop/iStockphoto, (meatballs) Sergey Ryzhov/Fotolia, (sauce) Chris Fertnig/iStockphoto, (mustard) Brent Hofacker/Shutterstock, (tomatoes) Patryk Kosmider/Shutterstock, (beans) Schlierner/Fotolia, (onions) Margo555/Dreamstime, (cheese) marco mayer/Shutterstock, (plates) Andrey_Kuzmin/Shutterstock; 70 (plates) Andrey_Kuzmin/Shutterstock; 72 (tl) Dionisvera/Shutterstock, (tc) Svetlana Kuznetsova/Shutterstock, (tr) bergamont/Shutterstock, (bl) Patryk Kosmider/Shutterstock, (bc) Zaneta Baranowska/Shutterstock, (br) Mediamix Photo/Shutterstock; 73 (tl) nicolebranan/iStockphoto, (tr) darren wise/iStockphoto, (bl) bonchan/Shutterstock, (br) bonchan/Shutterstock; 76 (tl) Gyorgy/Dreamstime, (tr) Sebastian Czapnik/Dreamstime, (bl) Aurora Photos/Alamy, (br) Pete Pahham/Shutterstock; 79 (t) cabania/Shutterstock, (bcr) Jorg Hackemann/Shutterstock, (br) Kokhanchikov/Shutterstock; 81 (tr) Supri Suharjoto/Shutterstock; 83 (tl) Manit Larpluechai/123RF, (tc) Barry Bland/Alamy, (tr) Evan Richman/The Boston Globe via Getty Images; 84 (bc) nicolesy/iStockphoto, (bcr) xavier gallego morell/Shutterstock; 86 (br) Lisafx/Dreamstime; 89 (tr) Eric Isselée/Shutterstock, (c) Ukrphoto/Dreamstime, (cr) Jakub Krechowicz/Shutterstock, (cr inset) HANDOUT/KRT/Newscom, (bc) dvdwinters/iStockphoto, (br) DEA/A. DAGLI ORTI/Getty Images; 90 (tl) Poco_bw/Dreamstime, (tr) Itinerantlens/Dreamstime, (cr) Dmytro Pylypenko/Shutterstock, (br) Jaimie Duplass/Shutterstock; 91 (cr) JOHN KELLERMAN/Alamy; 92 (cl) HANDOUT/KRT/Newscom, (c) Sylvain Grandadam/AgeFotostock © 2013 Artists Rights Society (ARS), New York / ADAGP, Paris, (tr) Katrine/EPA/Newscom © 2013 The Munch Museum / The Munch-Ellingsen Group / Artists Rights Society (ARS), NY; 93 (tl) Darren Baker/Shutterstock, (c) Stephen Lloyd Vietnam/Alamy, (cr) DEA/A. DAGLI ORTI/Getty Images; 94 (br) CREATISTA/Shutterstock; 96 (cr) Kesu/Fotolia, (cl) auremar/Shutterstock; 98 (tl) Blend Images/Alamy, (tr) Gyorgy/Dreamstime, (cl) Image Source/Fotolia, (cr) Monkey Business Images/Dreamstime, (bl) riekephotos/Shuttestock, (br) Sebastian Czapnik/Dreamstime; 102 (tl) Janos Csernoch/Alamy, (tc) dbimages/Alamy, (tr) amana images inc./Alamy

Printed in the United States of America

ISBN-10: 0-13-304503-X
ISBN-13: 978-0-13-3045031

16 17

Contents

BIG ENGLISH

♫ Song ♫

From the mountaintops to the bottom of the sea,
From a big blue whale to a baby bumblebee—
If you're big, if you're small, you can have it all,
And you can be anything you want to be!

It's bigger than you. It's bigger than me.
There's so much to do, and there's so much to see!
The world is big and beautiful, and so are we!
Think big! Dream big! Big English!

So in every land, from the desert to the sea,
We can all join hands and be one big family.
If we love, if we care, we can go anywhere!
The world belongs to everyone; it's ours to share.

It's bigger than you. It's bigger than me.
There's so much to do, and there's so much to see!
The world is big and beautiful, and so are we!
Think big! Dream big! Big English!

It's bigger than you. It's bigger than me.
There's so much to do, and there's so much to see!
The world is big and beautiful and waiting for me . . .
    a one, two, three . . .
Think big! Dream big! Big English!

unit 1

Every DAY

1 🎧 **Listen and match. Then sing.**

Kate Can't Be Late

It's Monday, 7:30.
Kate is still in bed.
Her mother sees the clock and says,
"Wake up, sleepy head!"

Go, go, go! Hurry, Kate!
Hurry, Kate! You can't be late!

"Eat your breakfast! Brush your teeth!
The school bus doesn't wait!
Now it's 7:45,
And you can't be late!"

(Chorus)

Kate packs her backpack,
And she combs her hair.
Now it's 7:55,
And her bus is there!

(Chorus)

Kate gets on the bus, and then
She sees that something's wrong.
She gets to school on time that day
With her pajamas on!

(Chorus)

a.

b.

c.

2 **Write. Then draw the time.**

I wake up at _____.

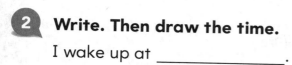

3 **What's missing in the pictures? Match and write.**
Use words from the box.

1.

a.

_____

2.

b.

_____

3.

c.

_____

4.

d.

_____

4 **Read and circle.**

1. four forty-five	**a.** 4:05	**b.** 4:45
2. five twenty-five	**a.** 2:25	**b.** 5:25
3. seven o'clock	**a.** 7:00	**b.** 6:00
4. two thirty	**a.** 2:13	**b.** 2:30

5 Read. Circle **T** for *true* or **F** for *false*.

I Love Mondays!

It's Monday morning and Dylan wakes up. He says, "Hooray! I love Mondays!" On Mondays, he has art class at 9:30. At 1:45, he has P.E. He loves P.E.! After school he plays soccer or basketball.

Dylan eats breakfast and gets dressed. He puts on his shoes. He's ready for school, but today there is no school! It's a holiday!

1.	Today is Monday.	T	F
2.	Dylan has art class after school.	T	F
3.	Dylan has P.E. at 1:45.	T	F
4.	Dylan plays basketball after school.	T	F
5.	Dylan is ready for school.	T	F
6.	Dylan goes to school today.	T	F

6 Continue the story. What happens next? What does Dylan do?

_____

_____

_____

7 **Listen and check (✓).**

At 4:00, Don
☐ goes to soccer practice.   ☐ does his homework.

At 5:00, Don
☐ plays video games.   ☐ plays basketball.

At 6:00, Don
☐ has a piano lesson.   ☐ eats dinner.

At 7:30, Don
☐ watches TV.   ☐ feeds the cat.

At 9:30, Don
☐ goes to bed.   ☐ goes to school.

8 **Write about you.**

1. What time do you wake up?   **2.** What time do you go to school?

_____   _____

3. What time do you eat dinner?   **4.** What time do you go to bed?

_____   _____

What does he/she do **before** school?	He/She eats breakfast **before** school.
What do you do **after** school?	I play soccer **after** school.

9 **Read. Then write *before* or *after*.**

7:00

wakes up

eats breakfast

washes her face

gets dressed

9:00

goes to school

does homework

watches TV

1. Susan eats breakfast _____ she wakes up.

2. She washes her face _____ she gets dressed.

3. She eats breakfast _____ she washes her face.

4. She gets dressed _____ she goes to school.

5. She does her homework _____ she goes to school.

6. She does her homework _____ she watches TV.

10 **Write the answers.**

1. What do you do before school?

   _____

2. What do you do after school?

   _____

11 **Look and read. Then write. Use the words from the box.**

| after | at | before | in the afternoon | in the evening | in the morning |

1. He plays video games at 6:00

_____*in the evening*_____ .

2. She wakes up _____

7:00 in the morning.

3. She washes her face

_____ soccer.

4. They ride bikes at 4:00

_____ .

5. She brushes her teeth

_____ bed.

6. On school days, I get dressed at

6:45 _____ .

12 **Look at** 11. **Then write about your day.**

1. _____

2. _____

Keep It Clean!

13 **Read and number the pictures.**

1. Wash your hands.

Your hands pick up germs. Germs can make you sick. After you cough or sneeze, wash your hands. Wash your hands before you eat.

a.

2. Take a shower.

Wash your face and body. Use warm water and soap. Wash away bacteria. Bacteria can make you sick.

b.

3. Brush your teeth.

Brush your teeth twice a day. Brushing your teeth cleans away bacteria. Bacteria can cause tooth decay.

c.

14 **Look and circle.**

Ways to Stay Healthy

1. (Wash your hands.) / Brush your teeth.

2. Take a shower. / Brush your teeth.

3. Take a shower. / Wash your hands.

4. Brush your teeth. / Wash your hands.

A sentence has a subject and a verb.

She eats breakfast before school.

She is the subject. *Eats* is the verb.

I ride my bike to school.

I is the subject. *Ride* is the verb.

15 **Underline the subject.**

1. <u>Jeff</u> wakes up at 6:45 in the morning.

2. We go to school at 7:30 in the morning.

3. I feed my cat before school.

4. Carol washes the dishes in the evening.

5. He plays basketball in the afternoon.

16 **Underline the verb.**

1. My sister <u>comes</u> home at 3:45.

2. He rides his bike to school.

3. They play video games after school.

4. My sister reads books on Fridays.

5. We make our beds before school.

17 **Write about two family members. What do they do?**

Family Members			
My aunt	My brother	My cousin	My father
My mother	My sister	My uncle	

1. _____ in the morning.

2. _____ in the afternoon.

18 **What chores do you do? Write. Use words from the box.**

clean my room   clear the table   feed the cat
make lunch   make the bed   wash the dishes

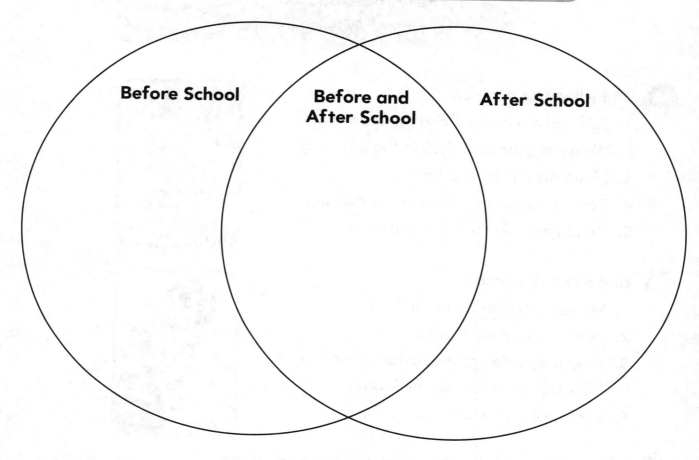

Before School

**Before and
After School**

After School

19 **Write about you.**

1. Before I go to school, I _____.

2. After I go to school, I _____.

3. Before and after I go to school, I _____.

20 **Listen and check (✓).**

	In the morning	In the afternoon	In the evening
1.			
2.			
3.			
4.			

21 **Look at 20. Write.**

> brushes his teeth　　gets dressed
> wakes up　　washes his face

1. On Sundays, he _____ late in the morning.

2. He _____ in the afternoon.

3. In the evening, he _____ and _____
before he goes to bed.

unit 2 In Our COMMUNITY

1 **Listen and sing. Then match.**

a.

♪ Community Helpers

There are many people
In our community.
We all help each other.
Helping is the key!

Community helpers help us all—
Young, old, tall, and small.

Firefighters, farmers,
Chefs, and cashiers, too.
Doctors, nurses, barbers—
Just to name a few.

(Chorus)

People work in restaurants,
Hospitals, and stores,
Fire stations, laboratories,
Indoors and outdoors.

(Chorus)

So next time you go out,
Tell workers that you see,
"Thanks for everything you do
In our community!"

b.

c.

d.

e.

f.

g.

2 **Choose one. Draw.**

Teachers work in a school.
Nurses work at a hospital.

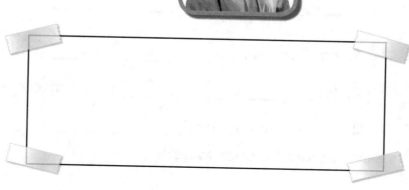

3 Listen. Draw the path and collect the letters. Then write the community helpers.

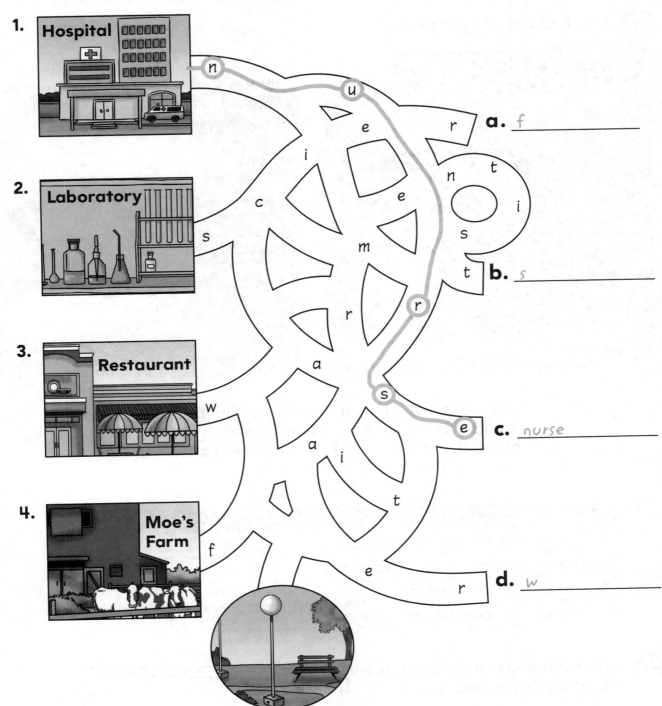

1. **Hospital**

2. **Laboratory**

3. **Restaurant**

4. **Moe's Farm**

a. _f_____

b. _s_____

c. _nurse_____

d. _w_____

4 Read. Write **T** for *true* or **F** for *false*.

1. A firefighter works on a farm.   **T**   **F**
2. A teacher works at a school.   **T**   **F**
3. A waiter works at a restaurant.   **T**   **F**
4. A mail carrier works at a post office.   **T**   **F**
5. A scientist works at a laboratory.   **T**   **F**

5 Read. Check (✓) *yes* or *no*.

Are You a Doctor?

A man is in a hospital. He is looking for help. He has a bad cold. He asks a woman for help. She works at the hospital, but she is not a doctor. She is a cashier. She works at the hospital gift shop!

	Yes	No
1. The man works at the hospital.		
2. The man wants to see a doctor.		
3. The woman is a cashier.		
4. The woman can help the sick man.		

6 What happens next? Continue the story. Write and draw.

_____

_____

_____

_____

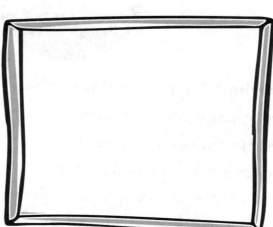

7 **Listen and check (✓).**

What does Peggy's dad do?
He's ☐ a cashier.   ☐ a teacher.   ☐ a barber.

Where does Peggy's dad work?
He works at ☐ a store.   ☐ a barbershop.   ☐ a school.

Where does Peggy's mom work?
She works ☐ at a restaurant.   ☐ at a police station.   ☐ at a barbershop.

What does she do?
She's ☐ a chef.   ☐ a teacher.   ☐ a police officer.

8 **Listen and circle. Then match.**

Where are they working today?

1. **A police officer / A firefighter**

a.

2. **An artist / A waiter**

b.

3. **A barber / A doctor**

c.

What does he/she do?	He/She is a nurse.
Where does he/she work?	He/She works at a hospital.

9 **Complete the dialogues. Write *do*, *does*, *work*, or *works*.**

1. **A:** What _____ your dad _____?
   B: He's a barber.

   A: Where _____ he work?
   B: He _____ at a barbershop.

2. **A:** What _____ your mom _____?
   B: She's a mail carrier.

   A: Where _____ she work?
   B: She _____ at a post office.

10 **Read. Write *Where* or *What*.**

1. **A:** _____ does your brother work?
   B: He works at a post office.

2. **A:** _____ does your sister do?
   B: She's a nurse.

3. **A:** _____ do you do?
   B: I'm a scientist.

4. **A:** _____ do your parents work?
   B: They work on a farm.

11 **Write about you.**

1. What does your mom or dad do?

   _____

2. Where does she or he work?

   _____

| What **do** your sisters **do**? | They**'re** (They **are**) nurses. |

12 **Write do, does, is, are, work, or works.**

1. A: What _____ your brothers _____?
  B: They _____ firefighters.

  A: Where _____ they work?
  B: They _____ at the fire station.

2. A: What _____ your sisters _____?
  B: They _____ nurses.

  A: Where _____ they work?
  B: They _____ at a school.

3. A: What _____ your dad _____?
  B: He _____ a waiter.

  A: Where _____ he _____?
  B: He _____ at a restaurant.

4. A: What _____ your uncle _____?
  B: He _____ a mail carrier.

  A: Where _____ he _____?
  B: He _____ at a post office.

13 **Read and match.**

Unusual Jobs

1. Mario is a storm chaser.

2. Dana is a fashion designer for dolls.

3. Ron is a video game tester.

a.

b.

c.

14 **Complete the crossword puzzle. Use the clues and the words in the box.**

companies	customers	designer	professionals
storms	unusual	video	

Across →

2. Mario drives near tornadoes and other _____.

4. Ron, Mario, and Dana all have _____ jobs.

5. Ron, Mario, and Dana are _____. They are good at their jobs.

7. Dana loves to draw clothes. She is a fashion _____.

Down ↓

1. Ron tells _____ about problems with their games.

3. _____ buy the video games.

6. Ron plays _____ games for eight hours a day. He finds problems.

15 **Read.**

Kids
Working Hard

Lalana lives in Thailand. She helps schools. Lalana and her friends ask people for books. They give the books to schools.

Carla lives in Spain. Carla and her big sister help tourists. Tourists visit Spain. They get lost. Carla and her big sister find the places they are looking for.

Marcus lives in Australia. Marcus and his friends clean up the streets. They pick up trash before school.

16 **Look at** 15. **Write.**   books   tourists   trash

1. Carla and her sister help _____ who are lost.

2. Marcus and his friends pick up the _____ on the streets.

3. Lalana and her friends give _____ to schools.

17 **Can you help your community? What can you do? Write and draw.**

I can help _____

_____

_____

_____

_____ .

A sentence can have a compound subject.
Al is a farmer. Pat is a farmer. → **Al and Pat are** farmers.

A sentence can have a compound verb.
I live in Rome. I work in Rome. → I **live and work** in Rome.

18 **Complete the sentences. Use names.**

We are sisters.

Rachel

I am a mail carrier.

I dance.

I sing.

I live on a farm.

Kate

I am a teacher.

I dance.

I play piano.

I live in a city.

1. _____Rachel_____ and _____Kate_____ are sisters.

2. _____ and _____ dance.

3. _____ dances and sings.

4. _____ dances and plays piano.

5. _____ lives in a city.

6. _____ lives on a farm.

19 **Write about you.**

I _____ and _____ in the evening.

My friend and I _____ after school.

20 **Write *do* or *does*. Then look and check (✓).**

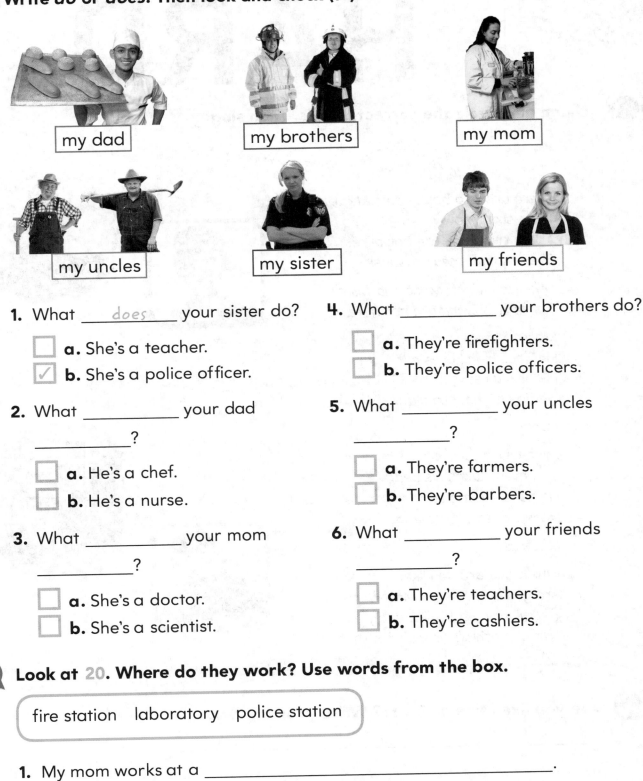

my dad   my brothers   my mom

my uncles   my sister   my friends

1. What _____*does*_____ your sister do?

   ☐ **a.** She's a teacher.

   ☑ **b.** She's a police officer.

2. What _____ your dad _____?

   ☐ **a.** He's a chef.

   ☐ **b.** He's a nurse.

3. What _____ your mom _____?

   ☐ **a.** She's a doctor.

   ☐ **b.** She's a scientist.

4. What _____ your brothers do?

   ☐ **a.** They're firefighters.

   ☐ **b.** They're police officers.

5. What _____ your uncles _____?

   ☐ **a.** They're farmers.

   ☐ **b.** They're barbers.

6. What _____ your friends _____?

   ☐ **a.** They're teachers.

   ☐ **b.** They're cashiers.

21 **Look at 20. Where do they work? Use words from the box.**

> fire station   laboratory   police station

1. My mom works at a _____.

2. My brothers work at a _____.

3. My sister works at a _____.

Working HARD

1 Listen and circle the correct words. Then sing.

♪ **Different Twins** ♫

There are two boys named Matt and Mike.
Their story now (begins) / ends.
These two boys are not alike,
Even though they're twins!

Mike and Matt. Matt and Mike.
These two twins are not alike.

Matt always messes up his room / cleans his room.
He does his chores each day.
He always studies for his tests / forgets his tests.
He has no time to play.

(Chorus)

Mike never cleans his room / messes up his room.
He never makes his bed.
He never wants to read a book / play outside.
He watches TV instead.

(Chorus)

Which one are you like?
Are you like Mike or Matt?
You might be a bit like each.
There's nothing wrong with that!

2 Are you like Mike or Matt? Write your answer.

_____

_____

3 **Draw lines to match.**

	Sun	Mon	Tue	Wed	Thurs	Fri	Sat

1. always

a.

2. usually

	Sun	Mon	Tue	Wed	Thurs	Fri	Sat

b.

3. sometimes

	Sun	Mon	Tue	Wed	Thurs	Fri	Sat

c.

4. never

	Sun	Mon	Tue	Wed	Thurs	Fri	Sat

d.

4 **Listen. Write *always*, *usually*, *sometimes*, or *never*.**

1. I _____ feed the cat.

2. I _____ study for tests.

3. I _____ take out the trash.

4. I _____ wash the dishes.

5 **Write two things about you.**

1. I usually _____.

    I _____.

2. I sometimes _____.

    I _____.

3. I never _____.

    I _____.

4. I always _____.

    I _____.

6 Read. Circle *T* for *true* or *F* for *false*.

I Have a Lot to Do

Brenda is thinking. She is making a list. She has many things to do before school. She has to eat breakfast. She has to get dressed. She has to brush her teeth. Then she has to feed her dog Hector, clean her room, and study for her math test.

Brenda goes to school at 7:50. Brenda's clock says 7:15. Her sister says, "It's 7:45." Brenda's clock isn't working! She has to get a new alarm clock! She has to run to school!

1. Brenda is busy before school.   **T**   **F**
2. Brenda has to clean her room before school.   **T**   **F**
3. Brenda goes to school at 7:15.   **T**   **F**
4. It is 7:45.   **T**   **F**
5. Brenda's clock works.   **T**   **F**
6. Brenda has to walk to school.   **T**   **F**

7 Write. What do you have to do before school?

I have to _____ before school.

8 **Listen. What do they have to do? Write and match.**

1. Tara _has to study_____.

2. Dave _____

   _____.

3. Christy _____

   _____.

4. Matt _____

   _____.

a.

b.

c.

d.

9 **Listen and check (✓) the pictures on the correct day.**

	Monday	Tuesday	Wednesday	Thursday	Friday
1.	✓				
2.					
3.					
4.					
5.					

What **does** he/she **have to** do?	He/She **has to** feed the dog.
What **do** you/we/they **have to** do?	I/We/They **have to** feed the dog.

10 **Read and circle the correct words.**

1. **A:** What **do / does** Nancy have to do after school?
   B: She **have to / has to** practice the piano.

2. **A:** What **do / does** we have to do this evening?
   B: We **have to / has to** study for our test tomorrow.

3. **A:** What **do / does** you have to do every morning?
   B: I **have to / has to** make my bed.

4. **A:** What **do / does** Peter have to do in the afternoon?
   B: He **have to / has to** go to soccer practice.

5. **A:** What **do / does** Gloria and Sam have to do today?
   B: They **have to / has to** feed the cat.

11 **What do they have to do? Look and write.**

Kate and Ted   **Jane**   **Jim and Mike**

1. Kate: _Kate has to make her bed._
2. Ted: _____
3. Jane: _____
4. Jim and Mike: _____

I/You/We/They	**always** **usually**	wash the dishes.
He/She	**sometimes** **never**	takes out the trash.

12 **Look at the chart and complete the sentences. Use *always*, *usually*, and *sometimes*.**

Family Chores	Monday	Tuesday	Wednesday	Thursday	Friday
1. take out the trash					
2. wash the dishes					
3. walk the dog					
4. do homework					

1. Dad <u>always takes out the trash</u>_____.

2. Peter and I _____.

3. Mom _____.

4. I _____.

13 **Read the question. Check (✓) the days. Then write the answer.**

Do you always clean your room?

Mon.	Tues.	Wed.	Thurs.	Fri.

_____

14 Read and complete the chart. Then write.

Weekly Allowance

Sam and Becca do chores. Their parents give them an allowance every Friday. An allowance is money that they earn when they do their chores. Sam wants to earn 5 U.S. dollars this week. Becca wants to earn 6 U.S. dollars this week.

Sam's Chores	Amount (in U.S. dollars)	Number of Times	Subtotal (in U.S. dollars)
wash the dishes	$1.50	2	$3.00
walk the dog	$0.50		
sweep the floor	$0.25	6	

TOTAL: $5.00

 How many times does Sam have to walk the dog? _____

Becca's Chores	Amount (in U.S. dollars)	Number of Times	Subtotal (in U.S. dollars)
do the laundry	$2.00	2	$4.00
sweep the floor	$0.50	2	
make the bed	$0.25		

TOTAL: $6.00

 How many times does Becca have to make the bed? _____

15 Write your chores and complete the chart.

Your Chores	Amount (in U.S. dollars)	Number of Times	Subtotal (in U.S. dollars)
	$1.00		
	$0.50		
	$0.75		

TOTAL: $8.00

16 Read. Then circle the chores.

Helping Out

1. Leah lives in Alaska. In the winter, it snows all the time.

   Leah has to shovel snow before school.

2. Ivan lives on a goat farm. His family makes goat cheese.

   Ivan has to get up at 5 o'clock in the morning to help his dad.

   He feeds the goats and gets the milk before school.

3. Chen Wei lives in Singapore. Her mother has a noodle shop.

   In the evening, Chen Wei does her homework.

   Then she has to help her mother make noodles.

17 Look at 16. Answer the questions.

1. Who does Ivan have to help?

   _____

2. What does Ivan have to do?

   _____

3. Who does Chen Wei have to help?

   _____

4. What does Chen Wei have to make?

   _____

5. What does Leah have to do before school?

   _____

18 Write about you.

1. When do you help your mother or father?

   _____

2. What do you have to do?

   _____

Use capital letters for most words in titles.

Walter and the Squeaky Wheels

Don't capitalize the following words in titles:

- *a, an, the*   Taking Care of a Big Dog
- *at, for, in, on, to, with*   Good Things to Eat
- *and, but, or*   My Brother and I

But if one of these words is first in a title, capitalize it.

The Big Blue Car

A Day at the Park with Grandma

19 **Circle the correct title.**

1. A big blue balloon
   a Big Blue Balloon
   A Big Blue Balloon

2. The Chef and the Waiter
   the Chef and the Waiter
   The Chef And The Waiter

3. Harry Needs a Helping Hand
   Harry needs a Helping Hand
   Harry Needs A Helping Hand

4. Dinner At Grandpa's House
   Dinner at Grandpa's House
   Dinner at grandpa's house

20 **Write the correct title. Use capital letters as needed.**

1. _____

uncle Joe's dream
Penguin trouble at the zoo
a Surprise for grandma

2. _____

3. _____

21 **Look at the chores. Complete the sentences.**

1. I have to _____ the piano on Tuesdays.

2. I have to _____ my room every Saturday.

3. We always have to _____ for a test.

22 **Look. Write *T* for *true* or *F* for *false*.**

Alicia's Chores	Monday	Tuesday	Wednesday	Thursday	Friday
make the bed	✗	✗	✗	✗	✗
wash the dishes	✗		✗		
feed the cat	✗	✗	✗	✗	
take out the trash					

1. Alicia always makes the bed. _____T_____
2. Alicia never washes the dishes. _____
3. Alicia usually feeds the cat. _____
4. Alicia sometimes takes out the trash. _____

23 **Look and write about Josh and Adam. Use *has to* and *have to*.**

	Josh	Adam
wash the dishes	✓	✓
practice the piano	✓	
study for a test		✓
leave for school at 7:00	✓	✓

1. *Josh and Adam have to* _____ wash the dishes.

2. _____ practice the piano.

3. _____ study for a test.

4. _____ leave for school at 7:00.

Think Big

Sue's Busy Day

1 **Choose one path. Draw the path. Learn about Sue's busy day.**

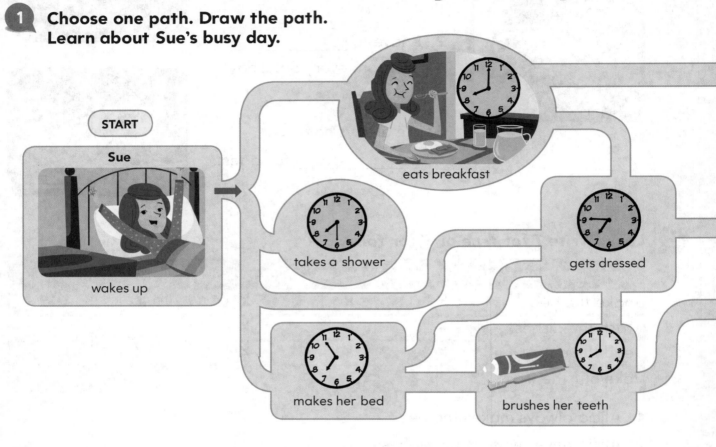

START

Sue

wakes up

eats breakfast

takes a shower

gets dressed

makes her bed

brushes her teeth

2 **Think big. Look at your path in 1. Guess and write.**

1. What time does Sue wake up? She wakes up at _____.

2. What does Sue do? She's a _____.

3 **Look at your path in 1. Write five sentences about Sue's day.**

_____

_____

_____

_____

_____

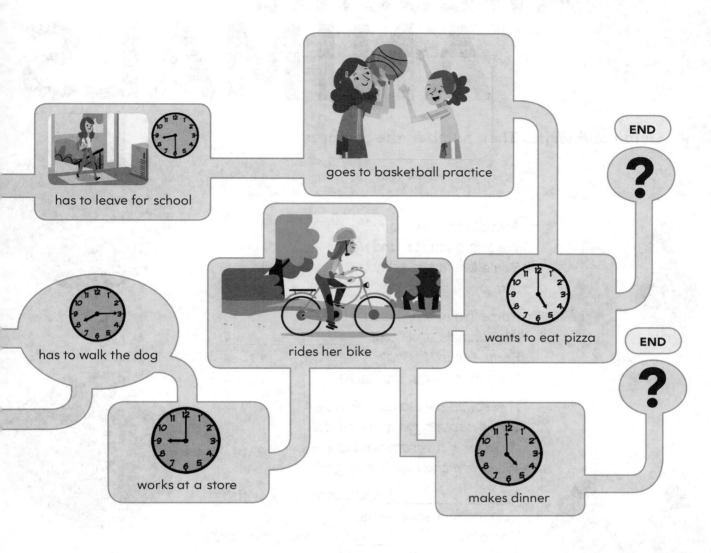

has to leave for school

goes to basketball practice

END

?

has to walk the dog

rides her bike

wants to eat pizza

END

?

works at a store

makes dinner

4 Guess and write. What does Sue do at the end of the day?

_____

_____

_____

_____

5 In Your Classroom

Work in a group and share.

unit 4 Awesome ANIMALS

1 Listen and write. Then number the pictures.

Animals Are Awesome!

Animals are awesome!
We see them far and near.
Some live in the forest—
Like owls, bears, and ¹_____deer_____.

Some live in the desert—
Like camels and some ²_____.
Some live in the water
In oceans, seas, and lakes.

Awesome, awesome animals—
What cool things you can do!
Awesome, awesome animals—
We share the Earth with you.

³_____ and other kinds of fish
Can swim in salty seas.
Parrots, ⁴_____, and other birds
Can fly above the trees.

Sea lions and ⁵_____
Can live in snow and ice.
Some animals are dangerous,
And some of them are nice!

(Chorus)

a. ☐

e. ☐

b. ☐

c. 1

d. ☐

2 Write.

My favorite animals are _____.
They live in _____.

3 **Look and number. Then color the animals.**

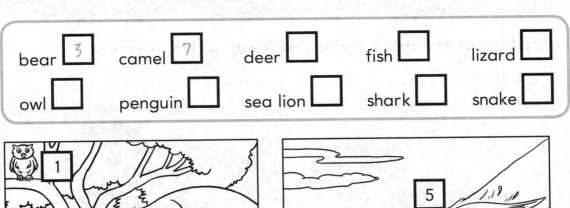

bear [3] camel [7] deer [ ] fish [ ] lizard [ ]
owl [ ] penguin [ ] sea lion [ ] shark [ ] snake [ ]

in the forest

in the ice and snow

in the desert

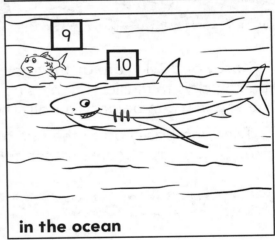

in the ocean

4 **Look at 3. Answer the questions.**

1. Where do bears live?

They live in the forest.

2. Where do sharks live?

_____

3. Where do penguins live?

_____

4. Where do camels live?

_____

5 **Read and look at the chart. Write *Yes, it can* or *No, it can't*.**

At the Zoo

Kasey and Tyler are at the zoo. They watch a sea lion. The sea lion can clap to music. It can't sing very well, so Tyler covers his ears! The sea lion can balance a ball. The sea lion can do many tricks.

Tyler and Kasey go to the parrot show. The parrot can ride a bike. It can say its name. It can talk! The parrot can't stop talking!

	Can it say its name?	Can it clap to music?	Can it ride a bike?
sea lion	_____	_____	_____
parrot	_____	_____	_____

6 **Answer the questions.**

What other trick can the sea lion do?

_____

Can you ride a bike?

_____

7 Listen to the animal quiz. Complete the dialogue.

Jonah: OK, this animal lives in the desert. It has four legs.

Pam: _____?

Jonah: Right! Your turn!

Pam: All right, this animal lives in the ocean. It can swim fast!

Jonah: _____!

Pam: OK, your turn.

Jonah: This animal lives in the desert, but it can also live in the rain forest. It can't run.

Pam: _____.

Jonah: That's right!

8 Match.

What can an owl do?

1. It can

2. It can

3. It can't

   a. hunt at night.

   b. talk.

   c. eat mice.

What can a fish do?

4. It can

5. It can

6. It can't

   d. climb.

   e. swim.

   f. live in water.

Grammar

What **can** a penguin do?	It **can** swim. It **can't** fly.	subject + *can / can't* + verb
What **can** bears do?	They **can** climb. They **can't** fly.	

9 **Look and write *can* or *can't*.**

1. Parrots and ducks _____ fly.

2. Parrots _____ talk, but ducks _____.

3. Ducks _____ swim, but parrots _____.

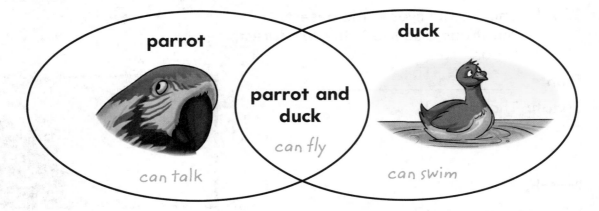

parrot

parrot and duck

can fly

duck

can talk

can swim

10 **Look and complete the sentences.**

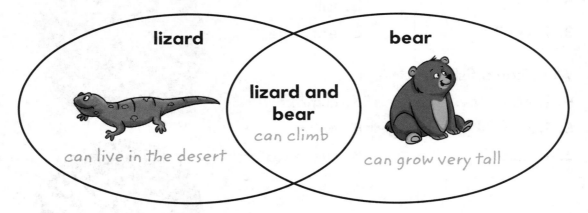

lizard

lizard and bear

can climb

bear

can live in the desert

can grow very tall

1. Lizards and bears _____.

2. Lizards _____, but bears _____.

3. Bears _____, but lizards _____.

Can a penguin swim?	Yes, it **can**.	subject + *can / can't*
Can bears fly?	No, they **can't**.	

11 **Read and circle the correct word.**

1. Can **bears** / **birds** fly? No, they can't.
2. Can **fish** / **lizards** climb? Yes, they can.
3. Can **ducks** / **camels** live in the desert?
   Yes, they can.
4. Can **parrots** / **sharks** swim? No, they can't.

12 **Write answers. Use the sentences in the box.**

No, it can't.　　Yes, it can.　　No, they can't.　　Yes, they can.

1. Can a bear climb?

   _____

2. Can penguins fly?

   _____

3. Can a shark sing?

   _____

4. Can ducks fly?

   _____

5. Can a sea lion do tricks?

   _____

13 **Read. Then check (✓)** *chameleon*, *polar bear*, **or** *stonefish*.

Animal **Hide** and **Seek**

chameleon

polar bear

stonefish

A **chameleon** can change its color and blend into its surroundings. It is hard to see.

A **polar bear** has white fur. It lives in the ice and snow. It is hard to see a polar bear in the snow.

A **stonefish** looks like stones in the sea. The stonefish is hard to see.

	Chameleon	Polar Bear	Stonefish
1. It can change color.	✔		
2. It lives in the snow.			
3. It can look like stones in the sea.			
4. It has white fur.			
5. It is hard to see.			

14 **Complete the sentences and color the pictures.**

1. A chameleon on a brown rock is _____.

2. A chameleon on a green branch is _____.

Pets in Different Places

15 **Match and complete the sentences.**

1. My name is Graham.

   I live in England. I have two pet _____.

   I like to take them for walks.

   They can run fast!

a. goldfish

2. I'm Mario.

   I live in Italy. I have a pet _____.

   It has soft fur. It's a popular pet in Italy.

b. parakeet

3. My name is Laura.

   I live in Mexico. We have a colorful _____.

   She can talk to us.

c. dogs

4. My name is Mei-Chun.

   I live in China. My family has a _____ in a bowl.

   It's a popular pet here.

d. rabbit

16 **Write about you. Complete the sentences.**

My name is _____. I live in _____. _____ are popular pets here. They can _____. They can't _____.

A topic sentence tells the main idea of a paragraph.
My favorite pet is my snake, Cornwall.

17 **Read. Circle the best topic sentence for the main idea.**

1. Main Idea: Polar bears are my favorite animal.
   a. Polar bears live in cold places.
   b. Some days are cold in the winter.
   c. I like polar bears.

2. Main idea: It's important to take care of pets.
   a. I want a pet parakeet.
   b. I feed and walk my dog every day.
   c. People all over the world have pets.

3. Main idea: Some pets can hurt you.
   a. My pet rabbit is white.
   b. Some animals are not good pets.
   c. Some animals can do tricks.

4. Main idea: The zoo is a great place.
   a. A parrot can talk.
   b. I always have fun at the zoo.
   c. Dogs are fun pets.

18 **Write a topic sentence for the following titles.**

1. My Favorite Animal

   _____

2. My Favorite Time of Day

   _____

3. An Unusual Job

   _____

19 **Look at the map of animals. Write answers.**

Animals of **South America**

parrot
(rain forest)

bear
(forest)

snake
(rain forest)

mountain lion
(mountains)

shark (ocean)

lizard
(rain forest)

penguin
(ice and snow)

1. Where can bears live? _They can live in the forest._ _____

2. Where can penguins live? _____

3. Where can parrots live? _____

4. Where can sharks live? _____

20 **Write questions for these answers.**

1. _____?

   No. Camels can't live in the ocean.

2. _____?

   Yes. Sea lions can live in the ice and snow.

21 **Read. Answer the questions with *can* or *can't*.**

1. Can snakes eat sharks? No, they _____.

2. Can a bear climb? Yes, it _____.

3. Can lizards sing? _____.

4. Can parrots talk? _____.

Sunny DAYS

1 Listen and write. Then number the pictures.

a.

□

Boring Weekend

It was a boring weekend.
I really had no fun.
No bike, no park, no outdoor games—
There wasn't any sun!

I finished all my homework
And read a magazine.
I made my bed and cleaned my room.
It's never been so clean!

Rainy weekends are no fun.
What's a weekend without sun?

All weekend it was ¹_____,
Cold, and ²_____, too.
I did some chores and read a lot.
What else could I do?

Now it's Monday, and it's ³_____.
It's a beautiful ⁴_____ day.
Too bad I have to go to school!
I can't go out and play!

(Chorus)

b.

□

d.

□

c.

□

2 Write about the weather and draw.

Today it's _____.

3 Match.

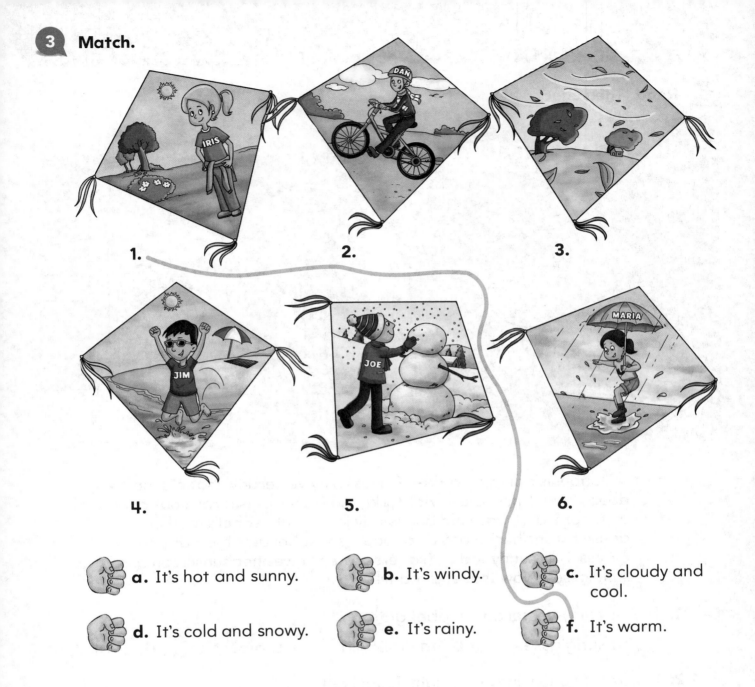

1.

2.

3.

4.

5.

6.

a. It's hot and sunny.

b. It's windy.

c. It's cloudy and cool.

d. It's cold and snowy.

e. It's rainy.

f. It's warm.

4 Look at 3. Complete the sentences. Use words from the box.

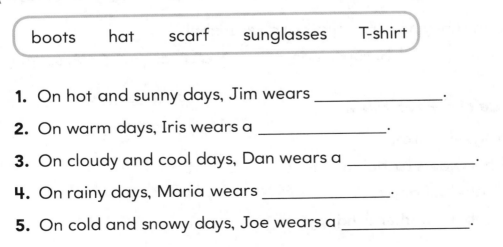

boots   hat   scarf   sunglasses   T-shirt

1. On hot and sunny days, Jim wears _____.

2. On warm days, Iris wears a _____.

3. On cloudy and cool days, Dan wears a _____.

4. On rainy days, Maria wears _____.

5. On cold and snowy days, Joe wears a _____.

5 **Read. Then check.**

All Kinds of Weather

Isabel is going on a hike. It was rainy yesterday. Isabel's mother doesn't want her to get wet today, so Isabel gets a raincoat and an umbrella. It was cold and windy last night. Isabel's mother doesn't want her to get cold today, so Isabel gets her hat and gloves. It is sunny today. Isabel's mother gives her sunscreen and sunglasses. Now Isabel is ready!

1. It was rainy yesterday. Isabel gets:

☐ **a.** sunglasses ☐ **b.** an umbrella ☐ **c.** gloves ☐ **d.** a raincoat

2. It was cold and windy last night. Isabel gets:

☐ **a.** sandals ☐ **b.** a hat ☐ **c.** shorts ☐ **d.** gloves

3. It is warm and sunny now. Her mother gives Isabel:

☐ **a.** boots ☐ **b.** sunscreen ☐ **c.** a coat ☐ **d.** sunglasses

6 **Circle *T* for *true* and *F* for *false*.**

1. Isabel is going on a hike.	**T**	**F**
2. Isabel's mother wants Isabel to get wet.	**T**	**F**
3. In the end, Isabel is happy.	**T**	**F**
4. In the end, Isabel's mother is happy.	**T**	**F**

7 **Listen. Complete the dialogue.**

Teacher: Hi, Jenny. How are you?

Jenny: Hi. I'm great! I went to see my grandparents in Florida.

Teacher: How was the weather?

Jenny: It was _____ and _____. There were flowers everywhere.

Teacher: How nice! It's so _____ and _____ here today.

Jenny: Yes, it is. I usually wear sweaters on _____ days.

Teacher: But today you're wearing a T-shirt!

Jenny: Yes. I like to wear clothes for _____ weather.

Teacher: You're home now. You have to wear _____ clothes.

Jenny: Yes, I know. I wore a coat and hat today, too.

8 **Look at 7. Read and write the answers.**

1. How's the weather today? _____

2. What does Jenny wear on cold days? _____

3. How was the weather in Florida? _____

4. What does Jenny like to wear? _____

9 **Write about you.**

1. On hot and sunny days, I wear _____.

2. On cloudy and cool days, I wear _____.

Grammar

How **is** the weather today?	It**'s** hot and sunny.
How **was** the weather yesterday?	It **was** windy. Leaves **were** everywhere.

10 **How's the weather today? Read and check (✓).**

 Bob

 Marco

 Sandra

1. Bob is wearing shorts and sandals.

☐ It's hot and sunny. ☐ It's cloudy and cool. ☐ It's rainy.

2. Marco is wearing a coat, hat, and gloves.

☐ It's warm and windy. ☐ It's sunny and hot. ☐ It's snowy and cold.

3. Sandra is wearing a raincoat and hat. She has an umbrella.

☐ It's sunny and cool. ☐ It's rainy and hot. ☐ It's rainy and cool.

11 **How was the weather? Match the puzzle and write.**

1. On Monday, ___it was rainy___ .   **4.** On Thursday, _____.

2. On Tuesday, _____.   **5.** On Friday, _____.

3. On Wednesday, _____.

12 **Read and look. Circle _T_ for _true_ or _F_ for _false_.**

Yesterday	Today

1. Yesterday the weather was cool.   T   F

2. It was not windy yesterday.   T   F

3. It's cloudy today.   T   F

4. It's cold today.   T   F

5. It was sunny yesterday.   T   F

6. It's warm and windy today.   T   F

13 **Look at 12. Write the answers.**

1. How was the weather yesterday? _____

2. How is the weather today? _____

14 **Write about you.**

1. How was the weather yesterday? _____

2. How is the weather today? _____

How's the **Weather?**

15 **Read and label the places.**

1. It is very rainy in **Lloró**, Colombia. It rains 13 meters each year.

Trees grow very quickly.

2. The **Lut Desert** in Iran is one of the hottest places on the earth.

It is so hot that not many people go there.

3. The **Atacama Desert** in Chile is very dry. It doesn't rain a lot.

It looks like the moon!

4. **Oymyakon**, Russia is very cold.

It is very snowy.

a. _____

b. _____

c. _____

d. _____

16 **Look at 15. Describe the year-round weather, or *climate*, in each place.**

1. Lloró, Colombia _____

2. Lut Desert, Iran _____

3. Atacama Desert, Chile _____

4. Oymyakon, Russia _____

All-Weather Sports

17 **Read. Then circle the weather words.**

Children around the world like to play sports in all kinds of weather.

1. On windy days, some children fly kites in Japan.

2. On rainy days, some children in Africa go swimming and play games in the water.

3. On cold and snowy days, some children go dogsledding in Alaska.

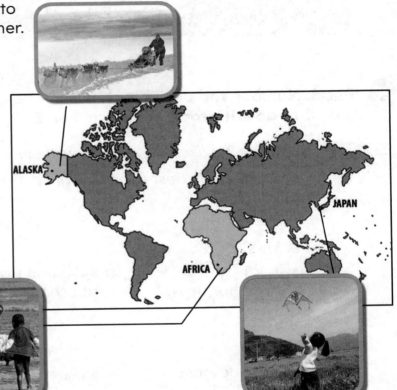

ALASKA

JAPAN

AFRICA

18 **Match the sentences.**

1. Some children fly kites
2. Some children in Africa go swimming
3. Some children go dogsledding

a. on rainy days.

b. on cold and snowy days.

c. on windy days.

19 **Do you like these sports? Write numbers to rate them.**

> 1 = I love it!   2 = I like it.   3 = I don't like it.

_____ flying kites   _____ riding a bike   _____ playing volleyball

_____ swimming   _____ skating   _____ playing soccer

_____ sledding   _____ running   _____ playing baseball

Here is a topic sentence.

My favorite season is summer.

After the topic sentence, give more information. Write detail sentences.

In the summer where I live, the weather is usually sunny and hot. I like to go to the beach with my friends. We swim or play volleyball. We have fun.

20 **Read. Number the detail sentences 1 or 2 to go with topic sentence 1 or 2.**

Topic sentence 1: *I like hot, sunny weather.*
Topic sentence 2: *My best friend is Julie.*

_____ **a.** I swim at the beach on hot days.

_____ **b.** Julie is in my class at school.

_____ **c.** She wants to be a chef.

_____ **d.** We play together every day.

_____ **e.** I like to ride my bike in the sun.

_____ **f.** I want to go to a desert.

21 **Write the best detail sentence for each paragraph. Use the details in the box.**

I walk Tiny every day.   Dogs were everywhere!   Math is fun.

1. Topic sentence: I have a pet.

Detail sentences: My pet's name is Tiny. He is a very small dog. He loves to eat ice.

_____

2. Topic sentence: Math is my favorite subject.

Detail sentences: Math is easy for me. I help my friends with it.

_____

22 **Look and complete the sentences.**

1. On _____ and _____ days, he wears shorts, sunglasses, and sandals.

2. On _____ days, he wears a raincoat and boots. He has an umbrella.

3. On _____ and _____ days, he wears a sweater and scarf.

4. On _____ and _____ days, he wears a coat, a hat, and gloves.

23 **Read the dialogue. Write _is_, _are_, _was_, or _were_.**

Emily: Hi Sam. It was fun to see you yesterday.

Sam: Yes, I had fun, too.

Emily: How's the weather this afternoon?

Sam: It ¹_____ rainy and cool. I took a walk this morning.
There ²_____ puddles everywhere!

Emily: It ³_____ cold and snowy here now.
There ⁴_____ mountains of snow.

Sam: That's funny! It ⁵_____ warm there yesterday!

Emily: Yes, but it ⁶_____ cold now.

unit 6 The Five SENSES

1 Listen and write. Then complete the crossword puzzle.

♪ ♪ Grandma's House ♪ ♪

I love to visit Grandma's house.
It always smells so nice.
It ^{1}_____ like ginger cookies—
Sweet, with a little spice!

Grandma smiles at me and says,
"I'm so glad you're here!"
Then she hugs and kisses me,
And calls me names like "Dear."

Yummy smells and her smiling face.
I really love my grandma's place.

Grandma likes to play old songs
From times when she was young.
The music ^{2}_____ so wonderful,
I have to sing along.

We always do my favorite thing—
Walking Mr. Chettham.
This dog ^{3}_____ cute and friendly,
So people stop to pet him.

(Chorus)

Crossword:
```
            T
            A
            S
     1      T
            E
  F  E  E  L  S
  3        2
```

2 Write about you.

1. What smells sweet? _____

2. What smells wonderful? _____

3. What tastes yummy? _____

3 Complete the sentences. Use words from the box.

> feels   looks   smell   sounds   tastes

1. My sweater  _____ soft.

2. This pie  _____ delicious.

3. This music  _____ pretty.

4. My hair  _____ terrible.

5. These flowers _____ nice.

4 Look and read. Then circle.

1. How does the apple taste? It tastes **delicious** / **bad**.

2. How do these shoes feel? They feel **soft** / **tight**.

3. How does my hair look? It looks **terrible** / **nice**.

4. How does the band sound? The band sounds **bad** / **good**.

5. How do the flowers smell? They smell **sweet** / **awful**.

5 Write.

1. How does the music _____?
   It _____.

2. How does the pie _____?
   It _____.

6 **Look. Then read.**

How Does It Taste?

Greg smells the fish soup. He thinks the soup smells bad.
He thinks the soup looks bad too. Maddie tastes the soup, and
then says, "It tastes OK." Greg tries the soup. He says, "It tastes
terrible!" Maddie has a cold. She can't smell or taste the soup!

7 **Write *Greg* or *Maddie*.**

1. _____ thinks the soup smells bad.

2. _____ thinks the soup doesn't look good.

3. _____ thinks the soup tastes OK.

4. _____ thinks the soup tastes terrible.

5. _____ can't smell or taste the soup.

8 **Listen and read. Write *true* or *false*.**

Mom: Alice, I have a new sweater for you.

Alice: Thanks, Mom. Oh! It feels nice and soft.

Mom: Do you like it?

Alice: Yes. I think it looks pretty. Thanks, Mom!

1. The sweater feels soft. _____

2. Alice likes the sweater. _____

3. The sweater looks terrible. _____

9 **Read. Circle the correct verb.**

Joe: Lily, something **smell** / **smells** bad.

Lily: Oh, I'm baking a hot dog cake!

Joe: A hot dog cake? That **sound** / **sounds** horrible. Yuck!

Lily: Do you want to **taste** / **tastes** it?

Joe: It **look** / **looks** OK, I guess. You **taste** / **tastes** it first.

Lily: It tastes awful!

10 **Draw an interesting or funny cake. Color. Then write.**

1. How does it taste?

_____

_____

2. How does it smell?

_____

_____

3. How does it look?

_____

_____

How **does** the apple pie **taste**?	It **tastes** delicious.
How **do** your new shoes **feel**?	They **feel** good.

11 **Read and match.**

1. They look pretty. They smell nice.

a.

2. It looks cute. It feels soft.

b.

3. It tastes good. It feels cold.

c.

4. They look hot. They taste delicious.

d.

5. It feels wet. It sounds nice.

e.

12 **Circle the correct word.**

1. How **do** / **does** the soup taste?
2. How **do** / **does** the shoes feel?
3. How **do** / **does** the music sound?

4. How **do** / **does** the pie taste?
5. How **do** / **does** the apples smell?
6. How **do** / **does** the shirts look?

13 **Complete the questions with *do* or *does*.**
Then look and complete the answers.

1. **A:** How _____ the sand feel?

   B: It _____ hot.

2. **A:** How _____ the birds sound?

   B: They _____ loud.

3. **A:** How _____ the dog smell?

   B: It _____ bad.

4. **A:** How _____ the hat look?

   B: It _____ pretty.

5. **A:** How _____ the sandwiches taste?

   B: They _____ delicious.

14 **Circle the words and complete the sentences.**
Use words from the box.

> delicious   great   nice   quiet   soft

Today Is a Great Day!

1. I am wearing my new clothes. They **look** / **sound** _____*great*_____.

2. My baby brother isn't crying. The house **tastes** / **sounds** _____.

3. I am taking a walk in the garden. The flowers **smell** / **sound** _____.

4. I am eating my favorite lunch. It **feels** / **tastes** _____.

5. I am playing with my clean cat. She **tastes** / **feels** _____.

Our Senses Keep Us Safe

15 **Read and circle the animal names.**

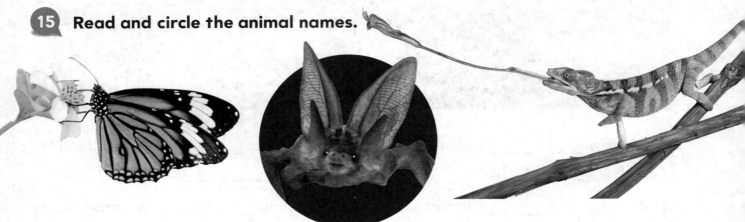

Animals and people have senses. They use their senses to stay safe. Animal senses are different than people senses.

(Snakes) and lizards smell with their tongues. Chameleons catch and taste food with their tongues. Butterflies taste with their legs. Bats use their ears to "see." They make a sound. Then they listen for the echo.

16 **Look at 15. Use the clues to complete the crossword puzzle.**

Across →

1. Snakes _____ with their tongues.

2. Butterflies _____ with their legs.

3. Our _____ keep us safe.

Down ↓

1. Bats use their ears to _____ things.

2. Chameleons use their _____ to catch food.

How Does Your Job Smell?

17 **Read. Circle *smell* and *taste*.**

I am André. I live in France. I bake pastries. They taste good and smell wonderful. I am happy!

I am Alberto. I live in Costa Rica. I grow and sell flowers. I like my job. The flowers smell nice.

I am Candace. I live in Canada. I pick up trash in the city. My job smells bad, but I like it.

I'm Sarah. I live in Singapore. I work at a zoo. I take care of Zelda the elephant. Sometimes she smells awful.

18 **Look at 17. Match and write.**

1. André tastes
2. Alberto smells
3. Candace smells
4. Sarah smells

a. flowers. They smell _____.
b. trash. It smells _____.
c. Zelda the elephant. Zelda smells _____.
d. pastries. They taste _____.

19 **Do you like these jobs? Write numbers to rate them.**

> 1 = I love it!   2 = I like it.   3 = I don't like it.

_____ Pick up trash.

_____ Bake pastries.

_____ Grow and sell flowers.

_____ Work at a zoo.

As you know, a paragraph begins with a topic sentence. It introduces the subject of the paragraph.

> I love tomatoes.

Detail sentences expand on your topic by giving details about it.

> Home-grown tomatoes taste delicious, and they are good for you.
> Fresh tomatoes right from the garden smell great.
> They look nice in a salad, too.

You end your paragraph with a final sentence. It expresses the same idea as your topic sentence but in a different way.

> Of all fruits and vegetables, tomatoes are my favorite.

20 **Read. Match the final sentence to each paragraph.**

1. My favorite animal is a dog. Dogs are friendly, and they can do tricks. They feel soft and look nice. They can't talk, but they can listen!

2. Butterflies are interesting. They look beautiful, and they can fly. They taste with their legs!

3. My grandma's house smells good. Her cookies taste delicious. She plays the piano. The music sounds wonderful.

a. They are my favorite insects!

b. It's a great place to visit.

c. They are wonderful pets.

21 **Write a final sentence.**

topic sentence → Lizards are amazing.

detail sentences → Lizards can run fast.
Lizards smell with their tongues.
Lizards usually feel dry and cool.

final sentence → _____
_____

22 **Look and circle the correct word.**

1. It **taste / tastes** delicious.

2. They **smell / smells** good.

3. It **feel / feels** hot.

4. She **look / looks** beautiful.

5. They **sound / sounds** loud.

23 **Complete the questions with *do* or *does*. Write answers about you.**

1. How _____ a butterfly look?

   _____

2. How _____ the rain feel?

   _____

3. How _____ your hair look today?

   _____

4. How _____ your shoes feel?

   _____

My hair looks bad today.

Max's Day at the Zoo

1 **Look at the paths for Max's day at the zoo. Complete the sentences. Use words from the boxes.**

ANIMALS
an owl
a shark
a snake

SENSES
sounds
looks
tastes
feels

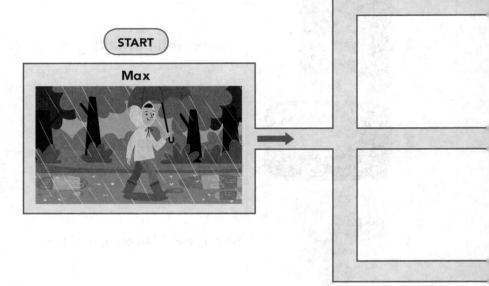

START

Max

2 **Choose one path. Draw the path. Learn about Max's day at the zoo.**

3 **Think big. Use your path in 1. What do you think? Write the answers.**

1. Animal Quiz

   It lives in the desert. It lives in rain forests.

   Some live in lakes and some live in oceans.

   It can't run, but it can climb trees.

   What is it?

   _____

2. How was the weather?

   Before the zoo, _____

   After the zoo, _____

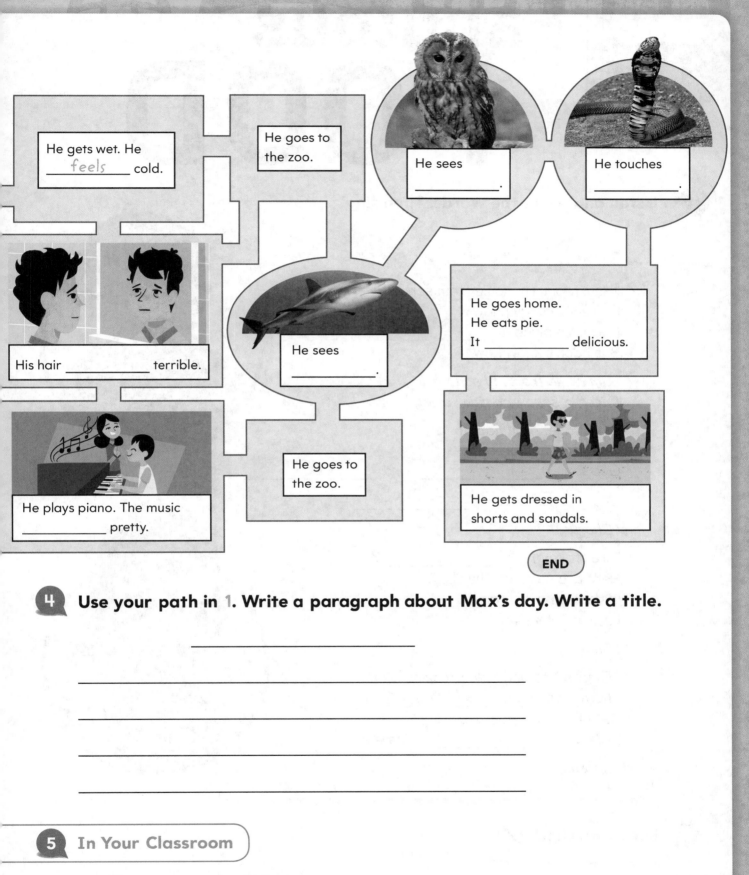

He gets wet. He _feels_ cold.

He goes to the zoo.

He sees _____.

He touches _____.

He sees _____.

His hair _____ terrible.

He goes home.
He eats pie.
It _____ delicious.

He plays piano. The music _____ pretty.

He goes to the zoo.

He gets dressed in shorts and sandals.

END

4 **Use your path in 1. Write a paragraph about Max's day. Write a title.**

_____

_____

_____

_____

_____

5 **In Your Classroom**

Work in a group and share.

unit 7 Fabulous FOOD

1 Listen and write the words. Then sing.

♪ Hungry After School ♪

"Hey, Mom, I'm home from school.
I'm really hungry now.
I want to make a ¹_____ ,
But I don't know how.

*I am home from my school day.
I need a sandwich right away!"*

Mom says, "You can do it.
It's easy. It's a breeze!
Get some ²_____ and ³_____.

Get yourself some ⁴_____."

(Chorus)

"Are there any ⁵_____?
Here are some on the shelf.
Is there any mustard?
I see it for myself."

(Chorus)

"There's just one little problem, Mom—
There isn't any ⁶_____!
But I have a great idea:
Let's have ⁷_____ instead!"

(Chorus)

2 Read and check (✓).

I like a sandwich with:

☐ pickles   ☐ lettuce   ☐ tomatoes   ☐ ketchup   ☐ mustard

Find and circle.

1. bread	2. cheese	3. green pepper
4. lettuce	5. mushroom	6. onions
7. pickles	8. pizza	9. tomatoes

4 **Look at 3. Write about you.**

I like: I don't like:

_____   _____

_____   _____

_____   _____

5 **Read. Then write. Use the words in the box.**

A Surprise for Mom

Lucy and Luke want to make dinner for their mother. It's a surprise. There is one green pepper, some cheese, and some mushrooms. The cheese and mushrooms are yummy. Lucy and Luke eat all the cheese and the mushrooms. Oh, no! What can Lucy and Luke make for dinner? They take out more food. Mom comes home. The surprise isn't dinner. The surprise is a messy kitchen. Lucy and Luke want to go out to eat!

| dinner | food | messy | mother | mushrooms |

1. Lucy and Luke are making _____ for their mother.

2. Lucy and Luke eat the cheese and _____.

3. Lucy and Luke find more _____ in the refrigerator.

4. Their _____ is not happy when she comes home.

5. Mom's surprise is a _____ kitchen.

6 Listen and match. Write *sandwich*, *soup*, *spaghetti*, or *pizza*.

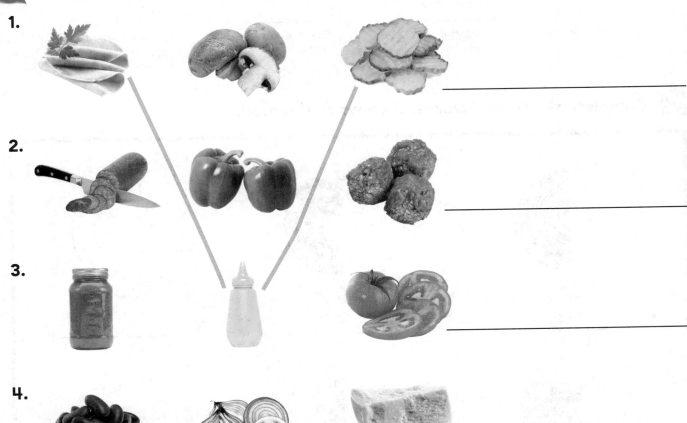

1. _____

2. _____

3. _____

4. _____

7 Draw your favorite foods and write.

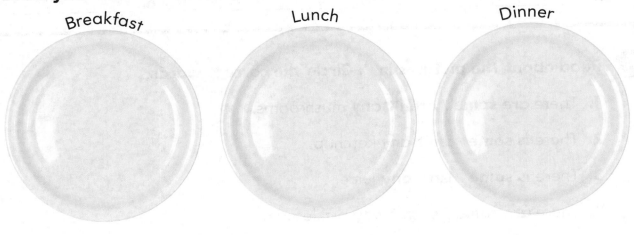

Breakfast   Lunch   Dinner

I like to eat _____

_____.

Grammar

| Is there **any** pizza? | Yes, there is **some** pizza. | Are there **any** onions? | Yes, there are **some** onions. |
| Is there **any** fish? | No, there isn't **any** fish. | Are there **any** eggs? | No, there aren't **any** eggs. |

8 **Complete the food pictures. Then write the food.**

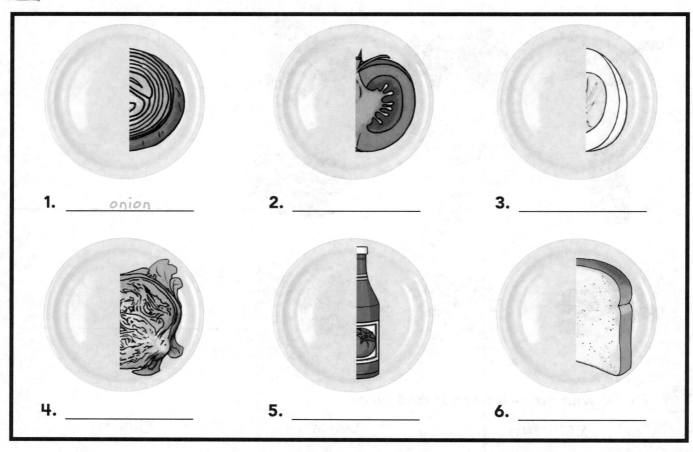

1. ___onion___

2. _____

3. _____

4. _____

5. _____

6. _____

9 **Read about the pictures in 8. Circle the correct words.**

1. There **are some / aren't any** mushrooms.

2. There **is some / isn't any** ketchup.

3. There **is some / isn't any** juice.

4. There **are some / aren't any** pickles.

5. There **is some / isn't any** lettuce.

6. There **are some / aren't any** green peppers.

10 **Look and write the answers. Use *some* or *any*.**

1. Is there any milk? _Yes, there is some milk_____

2. Is there any sausage? _____

3. Is there any ketchup? _____

4. Are there any eggs? _____

5. Are there any tomatoes? _____

11 **Look at 10. Write the questions.**

1. _____? Yes, there is some cheese.

2. _____? Yes, there is some mustard.

3. _____? No, there aren't any mushrooms.

4. _____? Yes, there are some green peppers.

5. _____? No, there isn't any pepperoni.

12 **Read. Then write A, B, C, D, or E.**

	Where Do We Get the Vitamins in Food?
Vitamin A	carrots, mangoes, milk, eggs
Vitamin B	potatoes, bread, chicken, cheese, eggs, green vegetables
Vitamin C	oranges, peppers, tomatoes, potatoes
Vitamin D	eggs, fish, milk, the sun
Vitamin E	nuts, green vegetables

1. Vitamin _____
2. Vitamin _____, _____, and _____
3. Vitamin _____

4. Vitamin _____
5. Vitamin _____ and _____
6. Vitamin _____

13 **Circle T for true and F for false.**

1. We get Vitamin A from mangoes.   T   F
2. We get Vitamin C from the sun.   T   F
3. We get Vitamin B from cheese.   T   F
4. We get Vitamin D from milk.   T   F
5. We get Vitamin E from oranges.   T   F

14 **Write and draw.**

I get Vitamin _____ from

_____.

15 **Read. Write the name of the person.**

Yoko is from Japan. In the morning, she usually has rice, soup, and fish. **Luis** is from Spain. In the morning, he sometimes has *churros*—small donuts. **Camilla** is from Mexico. In the morning, she usually eats huevos rancheros. **Tom** is from Australia. In the morning, he likes to eat toast with beans on top.

huevos rancheros

beans and toast

1. _____

2. _____

rice, soup, and fish

churros

3. _____

4. _____

16 **Look at** 15. **Complete the sentence.**

I want to eat _____.

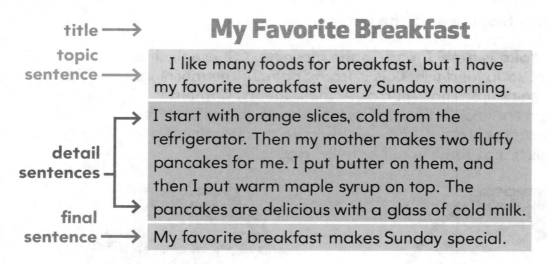

title ⟶ **My Favorite Breakfast**

topic sentence ⟶ I like many foods for breakfast, but I have my favorite breakfast every Sunday morning.

detail sentences ⟶ I start with orange slices, cold from the refrigerator. Then my mother makes two fluffy pancakes for me. I put butter on them, and then I put warm maple syrup on top. The pancakes are delicious with a glass of cold milk.

final sentence ⟶ My favorite breakfast makes Sunday special.

17 **Write. Use the words in the box.**

> title   topic sentence   detail sentences   final sentence

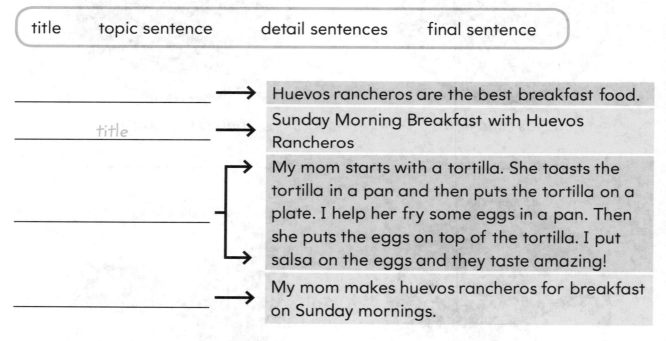

_____ ⟶ Huevos rancheros are the best breakfast food.

_____ *title* _____ ⟶ Sunday Morning Breakfast with Huevos Rancheros

_____ ⟶ My mom starts with a tortilla. She toasts the tortilla in a pan and then puts the tortilla on a plate. I help her fry some eggs in a pan. Then she puts the eggs on top of the tortilla. I put salsa on the eggs and they taste amazing!

_____ ⟶ My mom makes huevos rancheros for breakfast on Sunday mornings.

18 **Look at 17. Write the paragraph in order.**

Sunday Morning Breakfast with Huevos Rancheros

_____

_____

_____

_____

19 **Look. Then circle the foods.**

1.

The sandwich has:

bread	green peppers
tomatoes	pickles
ham	onions
cheese	lettuce
chicken	

2.

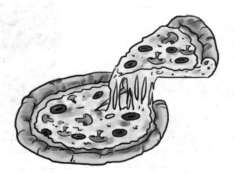

The pizza has:

mustard	lettuce
cheese	pepperoni
ketchup	pickles
chicken	mushrooms

3.

The salad has:

tomato sauce	pickles
ham	milk
lettuce	cheese
onions	chicken
green peppers	tomatoes

20 **Look at 19. Write the answers. Use *some* or *any*.**

1. Is there any lettuce in the salad? _____

2. Is there any lettuce on the sandwich? _____

3. Are there any pickles on the pizza? _____

4. Are there any onions on the salad? _____

21 **Write about your home.**

1. Are there any tomatoes in your refrigerator? _____

2. Is there any milk in your refrigerator? _____

Healthy LIVING

1 Listen and write. Then number the pictures in order.

Did you have breakfast?
I play video games.

Did you ride your bike to school?
I watched too much TV!

♪ ♪ *Get Some Exercise!* ♪

"Are you feeling well?" asks Mom.
"You don't look good to me."
"I didn't get much sleep," I say.
"¹ _____
_____"

♪ "² _____
_____"
Mom says, "You know I worry."
"Just a candy bar," I say,
"'Cause I was in a hurry."

Sleep right. Eat right.
Be healthy. Live right!

"³ _____
_____"
Mom says, "It's good for you."
"Dad drove me in his new car.
Mom, he offered to!"

"Let's ride bikes after school,"
Says Mom, "We'll start today."
"But Mom, I do get exercise.
I do some every day.
"⁴ _____
_____"
and stretch
My fingers as I play!"

(Chorus)

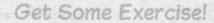

2 Complete the sentences about you. Circle.

1. I feel **great / awful / okay** today.

2. I **got / didn't get** enough sleep.

3. I **ate / didn't eat** healthy food for breakfast.

3 **Write. Use activities from the box. Check (✓) the healthy ones.**

> drank lots of water   got two hours of sleep   ate pie for breakfast
> rode a bike   ate a healthy breakfast   got ten hours of sleep

1.
□ _____
_____

2.
□ _____
_____

3.
□ _____
_____

4.
□ _____
_____

5.
□ _____
_____

6.
□ _____
_____

4 **Complete the sentences. Use _She_ or _He_.**

	Breakfast	Activity	Glasses of Water	Hours of Sleep Last Night
I feel awful!	candy bar	watched TV all day	2	5
I feel great!	eggs and toast	rode his bicycle	10	9

1. _____ is healthy.
2. _____ isn't healthy.
3. _____ did not exercise.
4. _____ did not drink enough water.
5. _____ ate a healthy breakfast.
6. _____ got enough sleep.

5 **Read. Answer the questions.**

A Healthy Dinner

Danny's dad wants Danny to be healthy. Danny likes unhealthy foods. He ate a big burger and French fries for dinner. Fried foods are not healthy. Danny drank a large soda. Soda is not healthy. It has a lot of sugar. Now Danny doesn't feel well at all.

1. Does Danny like unhealthy foods? _Yes, he does. He likes burgers, fries, and soda._

2. Are French fries healthy? _____

3. Did Danny drink a small soda? _____

4. Did Danny eat a burger and French fries for dinner? _____

5. Did Danny eat a healthy dinner? _____

6 **Draw a healthy dinner for Danny. Color. What is it? Write.**

_____

7 **Listen. Then circle.**

1. Olivia feels **good** / **bad**.

2. Olivia **did** / **didn't** get enough sleep.

3. Olivia **did** / **didn't** drink water for breakfast.

4. Olivia **ate** / **didn't eat** food for breakfast.

5. Olivia's dad **is** / **isn't** happy about Olivia's breakfast.

8 **Read. Then write *did* or *didn't*.**

1. Carmen: Are you feeling OK?

   Jack: I am tired.

   Carmen: _____ you exercise today?

   Jack: No, I _____. I played video
             games all day.

   Carmen: Oh. _____ you sleep eight hours?

   Jack: No, I _____. I slept four hours.

2. Ellen: Hi, Jim. I feel great today! How are you?

   Jim: Not good. I _____ eat a good breakfast.

   Ellen: What _____ you eat?

   Jim: I ate ice cream and I drank soda.

   Ellen: Yikes. What _____ you eat for lunch?

   Jim: I forgot lunch. I _____ eat lunch.

Grammar

9 **Look. Answer the questions. Use *did* or *didn't*.**

1. Did they get enough sleep? <u>Yes</u>, _____.

2. Did he get enough exercise? <u>No</u>, _____.

3. Did they get enough exercise? _____, _____.

4. Did she eat a healthy dinner? _____, _____.

5. Did he eat a healthy dinner? _____, _____.

6. Did she drink enough water? _____, _____.

7. Did he drink enough water? _____, _____.

10 **Write the questions. Complete the answers. Use _did_ or _didn't_.**

Poor Jonathan! He had a very unhealthy day.

1. _Did_____ he _____get_____
   enough sleep?

   _No_____, ___he didn't.____
   He only got four hours sleep. He's
   very tired.

2. _____ he _____
   breakfast?

   _____, _____. He had potato chips and donuts.
   But that isn't healthy, and he's very tired.

3. _____ he _____ okay today?

   _____, _____. He felt awful. And he's still very tired.

4. _____ he _____ a healthy dinner?

   _____, _____. He had meat and vegetables and fruit,
   and now he's not so tired.

11 **Look at the chart. Check (✓) the days about you. Then answer
the questions.**

My Habits Last Week	Sun	Mon	Tue	Wed	Thu	Fri	Sat
1. got enough sleep							
2. drank enough water							
3. ate healthy food							

Did you get enough sleep? _____

Did you drink enough water? _____

Did you eat enough healthy food? _____

What Is a Calorie?

12 **Complete the sentences. Use the words in the box.**

> a lot of   calories   riding a bike   watching TV

Your body needs ¹_____. Most people
need 1600 to 2500 calories every day. Dancing and
²_____ use ³_____ calories.
Sleeping and ⁴_____ do not use many calories.

13 **Look at the chart and the clues. Complete the crossword puzzle.**

Activity	Calories used per hour
sleeping	60
watching TV	75
walking	230
dancing	270
swimming	520
running	700

Across →

5. Four hours of _____ uses
240 calories.

6. One hour of _____ uses
520 calories.

Down ↓

1. Two hours of _____ uses
1,400 calories.

2. _____ for two hours uses
460 calories.

3. One hour of _____ uses 270 calories.

4. _____ TV for two hours uses
150 calories.

Strange Sports

14 **Read and match. Then write.**

Footvolley

Octopush

Pumpkin Regatta

1. In some parts of the United States and Canada, people play this sport. The people sit in pumpkins, and they race. This sport is called

_____.

2. People play this sport all over the world. It is like hockey, but players play it in water. Players use a small stick. They try to push a ball into a net. This sport is called

_____.

3. People play this sport in Brazil. They play it on the beach. They cannot touch the ball with their hands. This sport is called

_____.

15 **Read and match.**

1. Octopush is like hockey,

2. Pumpkin regatta is like a boat race,

3. Footvolley is like volleyball,

a. but the players do not race in boats.

b. but the players use a soccer ball.

c. but people play it in water.

16 **Make up a strange sport. Write the name and draw.**

The sport is called

_____.

Use *and*, *but*, and *or* to combine two simple sentences into one compound sentence.

I went to bed at 9:00. I woke up at 7:00.
⟶ I went to bed at 9:00, **and** I woke up at 7:00.

Dad ate oatmeal. Mom didn't eat breakfast.
⟶ Dad ate oatmeal, **but** Mom didn't eat breakfast.

We can walk to the store. We can take the bus.
⟶ We can walk to the store, **or** we can take the bus.

17 **Read and circle.**

1. I usually walk to school, **or** / **but** today
   I rode my bike.

2. Today I played soccer, **and** / **but** I walked the
   dog after school.

3. I can walk to school, **or** / **but** I can take a bus to school.

4. I like to play soccer, **and** / **but** I'm not very good at it.

18 **Read and write. Use the ideas in the box.**

but she sounds terrible
and I help her clean up
or I take the bus
but he isn't good at basketball

1. I help my mom cook dinner, _____.

2. My brother is good at playing soccer, _____.

3. My dad drives me to school, _____.

4. My friend always plays the guitar, _____.

19 **Write. Use the words in the box. Use *didn't* if necessary.**

ate a healthy breakfast	eat a healthy breakfast
get enough sleep	get exercise
got enough sleep	got exercise

1. John ____*didn't get enough sleep*____ last night.

2. John _____ this morning.

3. John _____ today.

4. Sue _____ last night.

5. Sue _____ this morning.

6. Sue _____ today.

20 **Circle the correct verb.**

1. Did they **eat / ate** a healthy lunch?

2. She **drink / drank** enough water today.

3. She didn't **play / played** basketball today.

Field TRIP!

1 Listen and write. Then match.

| aquarium | art museum | dancers | school | theater |

a.

Fun Field Trips

I like to go on field trips
And learn things out of ¹____school____.
We go to lots of places.
They're interesting. They're cool!

Today we took a field trip
To an ²_____.
We saw some awesome things.
We were glad to see them!

Field trips. Field trips.
They are lots of fun.
Field trips. Field trips.
Let's go on one!

Then we saw a show
At the ³_____ in our town.
My favorite part of it was when
The ⁴_____ twirled around.

Last year at the ⁵_____
We saw a penguin show.
We saw some scary sting rays
And some fish that glow.

(Chorus)

b.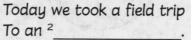

c.

e.

d.

2 Write.

My favorite field trip is _____.

3 Read and circle. Then number the pictures.

1. We went to a national park. We learned about:

   a. penguins   **b.** rocks   **c.** music

2. We went to the zoo. We saw:

   a. dinosaurs   **b.** elephants   **c.** paintings

3. We went to a dairy farm. We learned about:

   a. rocks   **b.** paintings   **c.** cows

4. We went to a concert hall. We heard:

   a. sea lions   **b.** some music   **c.** some cows

☐ ☐ ☐ ☐

4 Field trips are fun. Where can you go? What can you see? Write the places.

aquarium	art museum	dairy farm
national park	science museum	zoo

1. _____   2. _____   3. _____

4. _____   5. _____   6. _____

Story

5 **Read.**

The Awesome Field Trip

Megan and Marnie went on a school field trip. They went to the Red Rock National Park. They saw very old rocks at the park. They learned about many kinds of rocks. Megan liked the field trip a lot. Marnie didn't like the field trip. She thought rocks were boring. Megan got a present for Marnie. It was a rock!

6 **Look at 5. Write _Megan_ or _Marnie_.**

1. _____ really liked the field trip.

2. _____ didn't like the field trip.

3. _____ didn't like the rocks.

4. _____ got a present for her sister.

5. _____ doesn't like the present.

7 **Write one sentence about the field trip in Marnie's journal.**

Red Rock National Park
Field Trip

_____

_____

8 **Listen and write. Use words from the box.**

aquarium	bats
a concert	concert hall
science museum	sharks

1. Jason went to a _____. He heard _____.

2. Jason went to a _____. He saw _____.

3. Jason went to an _____. He saw _____.

9 **Read and match.**

1. We went on a field trip. We saw a play. It was really interesting.

a.

2. We went on a field trip. We saw beautiful paintings. It was really cool!

b.

c.

3. We went on a field trip. We visited a farm. We went an a hay ride.

d.

4. We went on a field trip. We saw bears, lions, and camels!

Where **did** you/he/she/they **go**?	I/He/She/They **went** to the Museum of Science.	
What **did** you/he/she/they **see**?	I/He/She/They **saw** an interesting movie about dinosaurs.	
Did you/he/she/they **like** it?	Yes, I/he/she/they **liked** it.	No, I/he/she/they **didn't like** it.

10 **Read and circle the correct form of the verb.**

Peter: Where **do / did** you go yesterday?

Lucy: We **go / went** to the zoo.

Peter: What **do / did** you see?

Lucy: We **see / saw** lots of animals.

Peter: **Do / Did** you like it?

Lucy: I **like / liked** it a lot! I love animals!

11 **Write. Complete the dialogue.**

A: Where _____ you go on your field trip?

B: We _____ to a dairy farm.

A: What _____ you see?

B: We saw farmers milk cows.

A: Did you _____ it?

B: No, I _____ like it at all! The cows smelled!

12 **Imagine a terrible field trip. Answer the questions and draw the place.**

Where did you go on your field trip?

You: _____.

What did you see?

You: _____.

What did you do?

You: _____.

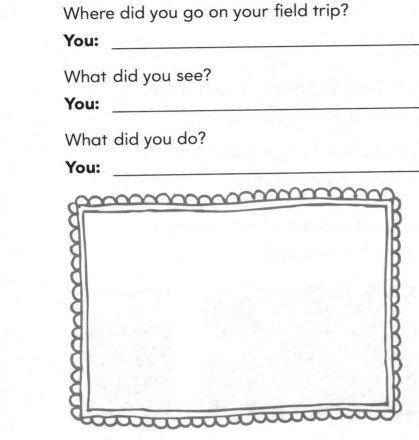

13 **Read and match. Make questions.**

1. What   **a.** did they go?

2. Did   **b.** did they see?

3. Where   **c.** they like it?

14 **Look at 13. Write the questions. Imagine the answers.**

1. A: _____

  B: _____

2. A: _____

  B: _____

3. A: _____

  B: _____

At the **Museum**

15 **Read. Then number the paintings.**

1. *Big Circus* is a painting by Marc Chagall. The painting is about things he remembers. The painting is funny and interesting.

2. *The Scream* is a painting by Edvard Munch. Is it scary? Some people think so. Is it strange? Some people think so.

3. *A Breezing Up* is a painting by Winslow Homer. The painting is about the sea. Many people think it is beautiful.

a. ☐

b. ☐

c. ☐

16 **Look at the paintings in** 15. **Write.**

1. *A Breezing Up* is about the sea. The painter loved the sea.
   Do you love something? What is it? _____
   _____

2. *Big Circus* is about happy memories. Think of a happy memory.
   What is it? _____
   _____

3. *The Scream* has a scary-looking man. Think of something scary.
   What is it? _____
   _____

The World Stage

1

2

3

17 **Look and circle the correct word.**

1. Flamenco is a   **a.** puppet show.   **b.** play.   **c.** dance.
   Flamenco is from   **a.** England.   **b.** Spain.   **c.** Vietnam.

2. Mau Roi Nuoc has   **a.** actors.   **b.** puppets.   **c.** dancers.
   Mau Roi Nuoc is from   **a.** England.   **b.** Spain.   **c.** Vietnam.

3. Shakespeare's plays were popular in the   **a.** 1900s.   **b.** 1800s.   **c.** 1600s.
   Shakespeare's first name was   **a.** Romeo.   **b.** William.   **c.** Tony.

18 **Write. Then check (✓) your answer.**

My favorite story is _____.

I want to see my story:

☐ in a dance.

☐ in a puppet show.

☐ in a play.

Writing | Subject-Verb Agreement

Read the sentences. See how the verbs agree with the subjects.

The girl **dances**.	The children **dance**.	She **does not sing**.	They **do not sing**.
The girl **danced**.	The children **danced**.	She **did not sing**.	They **did not sing**.

Read the sentences. See how the be *verbs agree with the subjects.*

I **am** cold.	He/She/It **is** cold.	We/You/They **are** cold.
I **am not** busy.	He/She/It **is not** busy.	We/You/They **are not** busy.

I/He/She **was** happy.	We/ You/ They **were** happy.
I/He/She **was not** sad.	We/ You/ They **were not** sad.

19 **Look and write sentences. Use the verbs in the box.**

are	is	isn't

1. (The children / at the aquarium)

   The children are at the aquarium.

2. The aquarium is fun! (It / a boring place)

   _____

3. (The penguin show / very interesting)

   _____

4. (I / a movie yesterday)

   _____

didn't eat	saw	was

5. (It / scary)

   _____

6. (I / my popcorn!)

   _____

20 **Write. Use words from the box. Then match.**

> art museum   concert hall   science museum   zoo

1. Many musicians played in the _____.

a.

2. The paintings are beautiful at the _____.

b.

3. We studied electricity at the _____.

c.

4. We learned about animals at the _____ last week.

d.

21 **Complete the dialogues. Use the *past* form of the verb in parentheses.**

1. **A:** My parents _____ to a play last night. (go)

B: _____ they like it? (do)

A: Yes, they _____! (do)

B: _____ you in the play? (be)

A: Yes, I _____! (be)

2. **A:** Where _____ you yesterday? (be)

B: We _____ to the museum. (go)

A: Did you _____ fun? (have)

B: No, _____. (do not) We _____ it. (not like)

Matt's Day

1 **Look at the paths for Matt's day and complete the faces.**

 = healthy    = unhealthy

2 **Choose one path. Draw the path. Learn about Matt's day.**

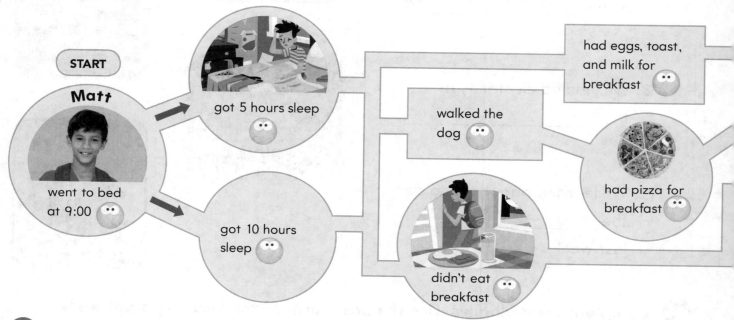

START

Matt

went to bed at 9:00

got 5 hours sleep

got 10 hours sleep

walked the dog

had eggs, toast, and milk for breakfast

had pizza for breakfast

didn't eat breakfast

3 **Think big. Look at your path in 2. What do you think? Write the answers.**

1. What time did Matt wake up? _____

2. Did Matt get enough sleep? _____

3. Did Matt get enough exercise? _____

4. Did Matt eat healthy food? _____

5. Where did Matt go on the field trip? What did he do? _____

_____

6. How did Matt feel in the evening? _____

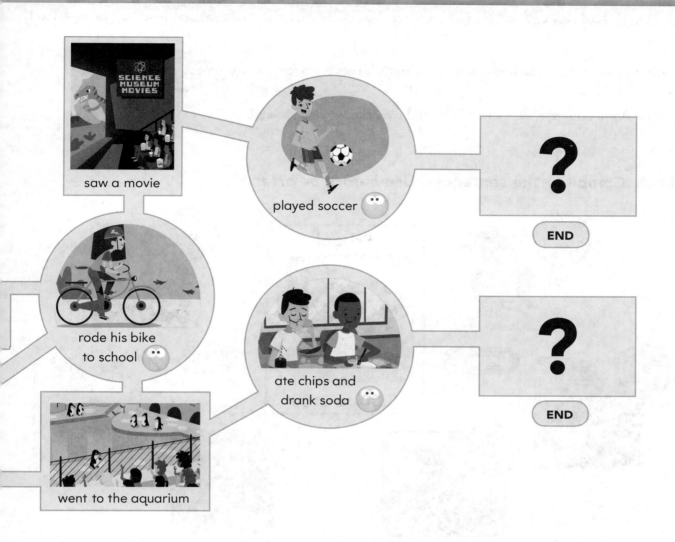

saw a movie

played soccer

? END

rode his bike to school

ate chips and drank soda

? END

went to the aquarium

4 Use your path in **2**. Write a paragraph about Matt's day. Write a title.

_____

_____

_____

_____

_____

_____

5 In Your Classroom

Work in a group and share.

What does he/she do **before** school?	He/She eats breakfast **before** school.
What do you do **after** school?	I play soccer **after** school.

1 **Look. Complete the sentences. Use *before* or *after*.**

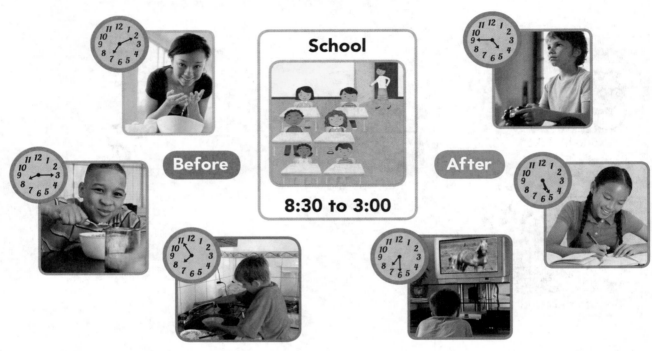

1. He plays computer games _____ school.

2. She always washes her face _____ school.

3. He always watches TV _____ school.

4. What does he do _____ school? He washes the breakfast dishes.

5. What does he have _____ school? He has cereal.

6. What does she do _____ school? She does her homework.

2 **Write about your family.**

1. What does your mother do in the morning? _____

2. What does your father do in the evening? _____

What does he/she **do**?	He/She **is** a nurse.
Where does he/she **work**?	He/She **works** at a hospital.
What do your sisters **do**?	They**'re** (They **are**) nurses.

1 **Look. Circle and complete the dialogues.**

Pete | Uncle – waiter | Dad – firefighter | Mom – cashier | Katrina | Dad – reporter | Mom – reporter

1. **Katrina:** What **do / does** your father do?
   Pete: He's a _____.
   Katrina: Where **do / does** he work?
   Pete: He **work / works** at a fire station.

2. **Pete:** What **do / does** your parents do?
   Katrina: They are _____.
   Pete: Where **do / does** they work?
   Katrina: They **work / works** at a television station.

3. **Katrina:** _____?
   Pete: He's a waiter.
   Katrina: _____?
   Pete: He _____ at a restaurant.

4. **Katrina:** _____?
   Pete: She's a cashier.
   Katrina: _____?
   Pete: She works at a supermarket.

What **does** he/she **have to** do?	He/She **has to** feed the dog.
What **do** you/we/they **have to** do?	I/We/They **have to** feed the dog.

1 **Look. Complete the questions and answers.**

All tasks
May 14
Matt to do: feed the cat twice today
Lucy and David to do: clean their rooms
Lucy and I to do: go shopping for new clothes
Lucy to do: practice piano after school

1. **A:** What does Matt have to do?

   B: He _____.

2. **A:** What do Lucy and David have to do?

   B: They _____.

3. **A:** What _____ Lucy and I _____?

   B: You _____.

4. **A:** What _____ Lucy _____?

   B: She _____.

I/You/We/They	**always** **usually**	wash the dishes.
He/She	**sometimes** **never**	takes out the trash.

2 **Look. Write *never*, *usually*, or *always*.**

Everyday Habits	Mon	Tues	Wed	Thurs	Fri
1. We _____ eat a good breakfast.	✓	✓	✓	✓	✓
2. She _____ plays soccer after school.					
3. I _____ wake up late.	✓	✓	✓	✓	

What **can** a penguin do?	It **can** swim. It **can't** fly.	subject + *can / can't* + verb
What **can** bears do?	They **can** climb. They **can't** fly.	
Can a penguin swim?	Yes, it **can**.	subject + *can / can't*
Can bears fly?	No, they **can't**.	

1 **Write one animal name in each box in the chart.**

a camel   dogs   a duck   lizards   penguins   a snake

What Can They Do?	Can	Can't
1. live in ice and snow		
2. do tricks		
3. live in the desert		

2 **Look at 1. Complete the dialogues.**

1. A: What can lizards do?

   B: They _____ in the desert.

2. A: Can a duck live in the desert?

   B: No, it _____.

3. A: What _____ dogs _____?

   B: Dogs _____ tricks, but a snake _____.

4. A: _____ a penguin _____ in ice and snow?

   B: Yes, _____, but a camel _____.

5. A: What _____ a camel _____?

   B: _____.

6. A: _____ a camel do tricks?

   B: _____.

| How **is** the weather today? | It**'s** hot and sunny. |
| How **was** the weather yesterday? | It **was** windy. Leaves **were** everywhere. |

1 **Look. Complete the questions and answers.**

 Janice

 Massi

 Yoko

Tegucigalpa, Honduras	
Yesterday	Today
32°C / 89°F	32°C / 89°F

Algiers, Algeria	
Yesterday	Today
23°C / 79°F	20°C / 68°F

Sapporo, Japan	
Yesterday	Today
10°C / 50°F	5°C / 41°F

1. **Massi:** How _____ the weather today in Tegucigalpa?

   Janice: It _____ hot and rainy.

2. **Yoko:** How _____ the weather yesterday in Algiers?

   Massi: It _____ cloudy.

3. **Janice:** _____ today in Sapporo?

   Yoko: _____

2 **Look at 1. Complete the dialogues.**

1. **A:** _____?

   B: It was hot and sunny.

2. **A:** How is the weather today in Algiers?

   B: _____.

3. **A:** How was the weather in Sapporo yesterday?

   B: _____. The snowflakes _____ everywhere.

| How **does** the apple pie **taste**? | It **tastes** delicious. |
| How **do** your new shoes **feel**? | They **feel** good. |

1 **Look. Match the words and write the sentences.**

1.    2.    3.    4.

1. The flowers   looks   awful. _____

2. The cheese   smell   tight. _____

3. The shoes   look   nice. _____*The flowers smell nice.*_____

4. The shirt   smells   comfortable. _____

2 **Write the questions.**

1. **A:** _____?

   B: The music sounds nice.

2. **A:** _____?

   B: The cookies taste delicious.

3. **A:** _____?

   B: The scarf feels soft.

4. **A:** _____?

   B: The perfume smells nice.

Is there **any** pizza?	Yes, there is **some** pizza.	Are there **any** onions?	Yes, there are **some** onions.
Is there **any** fish?	No, there isn't **any** fish.	Are there **any** eggs?	No, there aren't **any** eggs.

1 **Look. Write the food names.**

Special Today! Pepperoni Sandwiches!

_____

_____

_____

_____

_____

lettuce
mustard
bread
pickles
pepperoni

2 **Look at 1. Write *some* or *any*.**

1. There is _____ lettuce.

2. There aren't _____ tomatoes.

3. There isn't _____ ketchup.

4. There are _____ pickles.

3 **Write questions and answers. Then draw the sandwich.**

1. Are there _____ bananas?

   Yes, there are _____ bananas.

2. _____ onions?

   No, there aren't _____ onions.

3. _____ fish?

   Yes, _____ fish.

4. _____ ham?

   No, _____ ham.

Silly Sandwich

Did you/he/she/they **get** enough sleep yesterday?	Yes, I/he/she/they **did**.	No, I/he/she/they **didn't**.

1 **Find and circle the past form of the verbs. Then match.**

l	g	r	d	r	a	n	k	z
a	t	e	m	z	m	l	k	o
p	o	n	h	a	d	x	u	i
i	n	e	h	r	g	d	i	d
a	f	g	c	g	o	t	s	w
z	x	c	v	b	r	o	d	e

1. eat
2. do
3. drink
4. get
5. have
6. ride

2 **Look. Write questions and answers.**

1. A: Did Paul get enough breakfast?

   B: No, _____ . He _____ breakfast.

2. A: _____ enough sleep?

   B: No, _____ . He _____ enough sleep.

3. A: Did Linda have a big breakfast?

   B: Yes, _____ . She _____ eggs and toast.

4. A: Did Linda get some exercise?

   B: Yes, _____ . She _____ her bike.

Where **did** you/he/she/they **go**?	I/He/She/They **went** to the Museum of Science.	
What **did** you/he/she/they **see**?	I/He/She/They **saw** an interesting movie about dinosaurs.	
Did you/he/she/they **like** it?	Yes, I/he/she/they **liked** it.	No, I /he/she/they **didn't like** it.

1 **Look. Then circle the correct form of the verb.**

Jeff and Jack

Tim

1. Where did Jeff and Jack **go** / **went** yesterday?

2. What did they **see** / **saw**?

3. Did they **like** / **liked** it?

4. Where **does** / **did** Tim go last weekend?

5. **Does** / **Did** Tim like it?

2 **Look at 1. Write the answers.**

1. Jeff and Jack _____ yesterday.

2. _____ a play.

3. No, _____ it.

4. He _____.

5. Yes, _____ it a lot.

My BIG ENGLISH World

Workbook **3**

My name: _____

My age: _____

My address: _____

My family: _____

ME

ENGLISH

AROUND ME

Look around you. Paste or draw things with English words. Write everyday words.

Everyday Words

MOVIE TICKET

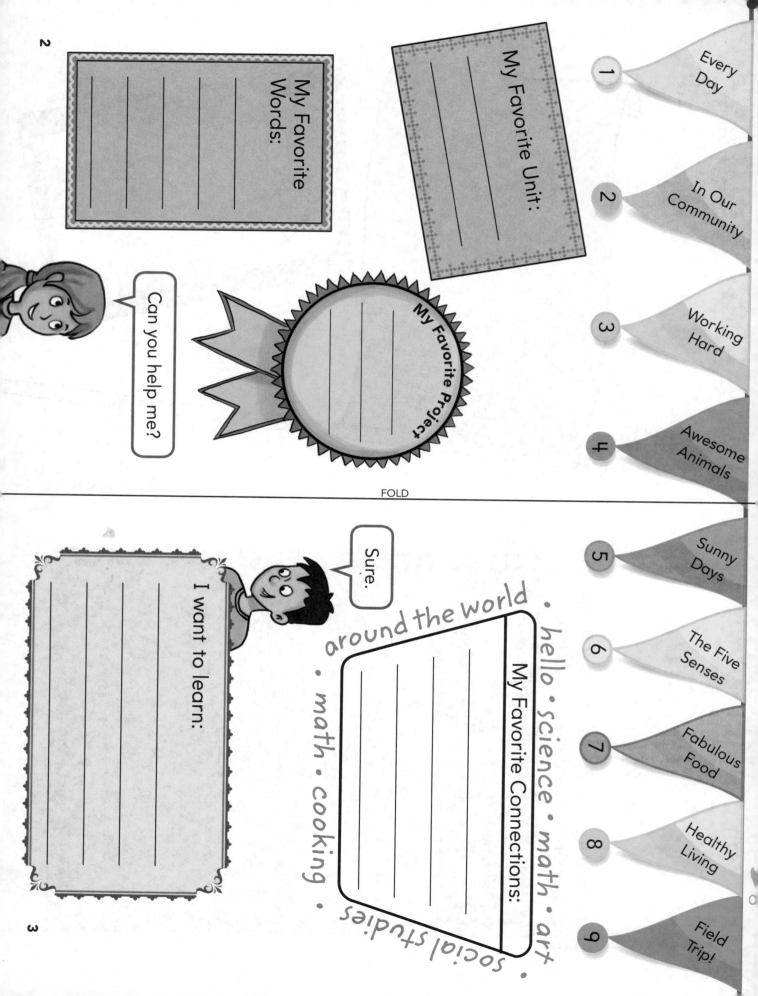

My Favorite Unit: _____

My Favorite Words: _____

My Favorite Project _____

Can you help me?

1 Every Day

2 In Our Community

3 Working Hard

4 Awesome Animals

FOLD

I want to learn: _____

Sure.

My Favorite Connections: _____

• hello • science • math • art • around the world • math • cooking • social studies •

5 Sunny Days

6 The Five Senses

7 Fabulous Food

8 Healthy Living

9 Field Trip!

2

3